All The Rivers Run Into The Sea

Also by Kathleen Stauffer

We See In A Mirror Dimly

The Secret Is

ALL THE
Rivers
RUN INTO THE
Sea

Kathleen Stauffer

WestBow
PRESS
A DIVISION OF THOMAS NELSON

WestBow Press books may be ordered through booksellers or by contacting:

WestBow Press
A Division of Thomas Nelson
1663 Liberty Drive
Bloomington, IN 47403
www.westbowpress.com
1-(866) 928-1240

Because of the dynamic nature of the Internet, any web addresses or links contained in this book may have changed since publication and may no longer be valid. The views expressed in this work are solely those of the author and do not necessarily reflect the views of the publisher, and the publisher hereby disclaims any responsibility for them.

Any people depicted in stock imagery provided by Thinkstock are models, and such images are being used for illustrative purposes only.

Certain stock imagery © Thinkstock.

ISBN: 978-1-4497-1117-7 (sc)
ISBN: 978-1-4497-1118-4 (dj)
ISBN: 978-1-4497-1119-1 (e)

Library of Congress Control Number: 2011927018

Scripture references taken from the Holy Bible, Revised Standard Version, Thomas Nelson and Sons, New York, 1953.

Scripture references taken from the Good News Testament, American Bible Society, 1976 (The New Testament in Today's English Version).

Printed in the United States of America

WestBow Press rev. date: 4/22/2011

This book is dedicated to my father,
Carl Abel,
. . . always an inspiration for me.

My sincere appreciation to "first readers" Ann Hanson and Heidi Feekes; to Margaret Smolik, editor; and to Susie Brandau, for her technological expertise.

Thank you, David, for being you.
Luabc

To everything there is a season, and a time to every purpose under the heaven. A time to be born, and a time to die; a time to plant, and a time to pluck up what is planted; a time to kill, and a time to heal; a time to break down, and a time to build up; a time to weep, and a time to laugh; a time to mourn, and a time to dance; a time to cast away stones, and a time to gather stones together; a time to embrace, and a time to refrain from embracing; a time to seek, and a time to lose; a time to keep, and a time to cast away; a time to rend, and a time to sew; a time to keep silence, and a time to speak; a time to love, and a time to hate; a time for war, and a time for peace.

What gain has the worker from his toil? I have seen the business that God has given to the sons of men to be busy with. He has made everything beautiful in its time....

Ecclesiastes 3: 1 - 11

Prologue

We meet persons during our lives who affect us for the rest of our lives whether we want them to or not. For me, it was Bill; and then it was Martin; and then it was Dan; and then it was. . . . .

You see how it goes. At times we find ourselves longing for someone or something that is not. Before you read this novel, I want you to ask yourself what love is. God is love, and we are created in his image; we were made to love.

My friend, Dorcas, a writer, once wondered if many of our dilemmas are caused by "running from our inner loneliness....a major human experience." We all desire lasting relationships, and yet we are "looking at our world suspiciously...and expect an enemy to appear and do us harm." Perhaps we do not know how to love; perhaps when we are not right with God, we cannot be right with others.

I suppose it's all a part of our sinful human nature. Dorcas feels we have "immense opportunities to remove weeds and stones that prevent change of heart and mind." If I had known then what I know now, would my life have been different? Rhetorical question, of course. We all start as children.

1

Baby Boomers, it's what they called our generation. Feeling in the way while the staff dressed my mom in a gown and placed her in a make-shift bed next to the elevator, Dad prepared to leave the hospital. Mom kissed him goodbye, told him to get something to eat; she would be fine. My mother looked around—pregnant women, harried nurses and babies everywhere. There was indeed no room in the inn. When Dad returned a couple of hours later, she told him they had a baby girl. Because her bed was still by the elevator, he didn't believe her. The nurse walked him to the nursery where she pointed out a chubby, dark-haired girl and convinced him otherwise. Meaning *pure one,* Karen was to be my name.

It was 1947. Another world war was history. President Harry Truman was in office with no vice-president. The first of the Dead Sea Scrolls had been discovered, and a series of forest fires had burned millions of dollars worth of timber in the New England states. However, my parents brought me home to a house with no running water, two little brothers, and a farm to run; so not knowing the news on a day by day basis was not even an inconvenience.

I have few early childhood memories: older brothers playing on the floor next to a large, somewhat splintery, wooden toy box; a hot summer spent on an old army cot on the screened-in porch off the kitchen with chicken pocks and then the mumps; cold drafts in the deep of winter and bare feet in mud puddles after an August thunderstorm. I remember a picture of us kids dressed in seersucker outfits made by Mom. We swam on summer Sundays in a nearby lake and ate fried chicken and white bread smothered with butter after leaving the water with shivers and a good appetite. Perhaps those early experiences gave me a love for water—lakes, streams, wading pools, puddles after a downpour.

I remember as an older child visiting Lake Itasca in north-central Minnesota with my family. I must have been seven or eight. We waded across a little stream about eighteen feet wide and less than a foot deep. Many others were there. Some of the children were carried on their parents' shoulders. Sounds of cameras clicking and conversation filled the air. When Dad explained that eventually this stream would develop into a mighty river which in some places would be a mile across and 100 feet deep, my brothers and I looked at our mother with a can-this-be true expression. Mom smiled that knowing smile of hers and nodded.

In our family tent that night at a KOA camping ground, Mom told us the story of Fannie, our great grandmother. Zipped up in cozy sleeping bags with a lantern softly burning in the tent corner, Mom quietly filled us in on some fascinating family history. Sometime during the 1850's, my great grandfather was on his way to California in search of gold. He met a beautiful, dark-haired, dark-eyed woman—the daughter of an Indian family living close to The Great River. Mom didn't know the details of how they met or fell in love, but Fannie, Grandpa's name for her, left her home and family and went to California with my great grandpa. They had two children. One son died in a hunting accident, and the other one left at a young age to become a trapper on the Mississippi. Because Great Grandpa couldn't deal with losing two sons, he left Fannie, their mother, and headed to Silver City, Idaho, where he got into a lot of trouble. Unable to support herself and very lonely, Fannie returned to the tribe she had left so many years before. Explorers and trappers reported a woman of her description canoeing on the Mississippi. Mom told us that Fannie means "free one," and Mom hoped that our great grandmother found some kind of peace by returning to her roots and her own people.

It was a fidgety night for me. Thinking my great grandmother was a beautiful Indian princess and, besides that, loved the water—just like me—lit a fire in my already active imagination.

After that particular family trip, the M I S S I S S I P P I school-yard chant that rolled off our tongues during jump rope sessions had a special meaning. I would recall the photo of me in a multi colored tank top and aqua colored shorts standing huddled together with my family near the Lake Itasca stream with goofy grins on our faces.

Whenever I had an opportunity to day-dream, the story about Fannie, my great grandmother, came to mind along with a hundred possibilities of what her life might have been like and any implication it might have for me. Watching the sun sparkle off the water, shading my eyes and looking downstream, I had felt the mystery.

Because of this love of the water, later in life, I began to think of life (especially my own) like a river. Everyone comes from God and returns to God. Perhaps there is no death—only another beginning. With all of its twists and irregularities, a river is fascinating, yet unpredictable. And, the path of the river is always changing. As is life.

Mark Twain wrote, "The river is a *wonderful* book with a new story to tell every day." According to a high school graduation gift, the 1965 Webster's New Collegiate Dictionary, *wonderful* means marvelous, admirable, astonishing.

"… far beyond anything previously known or anticipated," one of the meanings of the word *wonders*, I consider a better definition, and, like Mark Twain, I do have a story to tell.

I've informed my birthday club group to start shopping for swimwear. The year I turn 70, we're all headed to the nearest in-door water park—my treat. Or, we will rent a houseboat on the river, enjoy luscious food, share memories, and drift down the river on a lazy afternoon. Maybe, we'll do both.

Meanwhile, my story…

2

My childhood was a normal childhood only if you call *normal* having two loving, working parents; family vacations; tickling, laughter, jumping on the bed; and a warm, safe place to sleep each night after both Mom and Dad tucked us in with a kiss and a prayer. I thank God for that. I thank God because the unconditional love my parents gave enabled me to understand the magnitude of God's love. As a child, I accepted God's love as a given. God created the world. God loved us. We loved God. Only as an adult would I truly understand the depths of God's love, grace, and forgiveness.

Everything, of course, was not perfect. We had the occasional sibling fight and many times had poor attitudes about the farm work. And around five years old, I started worrying about the boogey man under my bed. I'd check every night; after all, you don't want to go to bed with the boogey man underneath your bed. Who knows what might happen during the night. There was a problem with checking, however. My boogey man was quick. As soon as I looked under the bed, I was sure he had slithered to my closet. And so it went, the nightly ritual, back and forth, from closet to under the bed. It was exhausting. I never caught him. I outgrew this nasty fear although I'm not sure at what age; however, I did think about the boogey man later in life.

I grew up on a farm with chickens, cattle, hogs, an occasional horse, and corn and soybeans to be harvested each fall. There was a routine to everything. Before I climbed out of bed in the morning, I could hear the clatter of pots downstairs in the kitchen as Mom started to prepare breakfast. If I looked out of the window a foot from the end of my bed, I could often see my dad walking from the corncrib to the hog house carrying buckets of feed. If I lingered a bit longer, the smell of frying bacon drifted up the steps, and I knew there would soon be eggs in the pan where the bacon had been.

On Mondays, in the basement, we sorted the laundry that had dropped down the chute during the previous week. It was always a huge pile and would have been fun to jump into if not for the smell. There were white-whites, light colored clothing, dark clothes, jeans and chore clothes, and towels all sorted in different piles. Some piles were waist high. The NORGE washer was filled with a hose: hot for the first cycle, then a warm rinse, then a cold rinse in the final tub. A hand-fed ringer pulled the clothing from one tub to another until everything was clean and rinsed. If Mom ran the ringer, I carried the wet clothes in a plastic-lined bushel basket up the basement steps and out to the clothesline. I liked hanging the towels or shirts, connecting them with clothes pins, putting like colors and sizes together. It was a good feeling to step back and look at my creation with the morning sun gently warming my face and shoulders. A gentle breeze added the right touch.

On other days, there were chickens to butcher, sweet corn to can, or apples to pick from the trees next to our house and make into applesauce. The days were always full. During harvesting, my uncle and cousins would come to help since we shared farm equipment. Mom and I would start early. A roast was put in the oven, a pie crust was rolled out, potatoes were peeled. Soon after dinner and a mountain of dishes, the preparation would begin again for an afternoon lunch: cold meat sandwiches, chips and Kool-Aid mixed with orange juice. Mom must have thought it to be healthy. I remember asking her if we could just have *plain* Kool-Aid. That would have been a treat. It only happened on days we were out of frozen OJ.

During summer vacations, we attended Bible school and swimming lessons. I tasted my first chocolate milk from a carton at Bible school. Chocolate milk brings back memories of sweaty kids in church classrooms learning Bible verses. Swimming lessons were a little more fun. I loved the water. Although I struggled as a beginner, I was a determined learner and soon passed the deep end test. I liked diving into the water, treading, swimming, all of it. Floating on my back, I would look into the sky with the sounds of underwater gurgling and other children's muted conversations in my head thinking about nothing. Nothing. Thousands of miles away, the sky was crystal blue.

Even as I grew older, and it was not cool to go swimming, I would go on my own whenever I had the chance. A lake, a pool, a creek to wade in— it didn't matter. If we traveled and there was a stream, my feet would end up in it. On rainy days, while others lingered indoors waiting for the rain to stop, I felt pulled to be outdoors—face-up, getting drenched, watching the wind whip the tree branches while listening to the sky grumble.

During the school year, the routine varied a little. Mom was always in the kitchen when my brothers and I arrived home. Taking the back steps to our old farmhouse two at a time, we were greeted by the smell of a favorite hot dish or homemade soup that made us eager for supper. There was always homemade bread, chocolate chip cookies in the cookie jar and chocolate cake with fudge frosting for dessert. After a quick snack and changing clothes, we were off to do chores or homework.

In sixth grade I remember diligently working on a report about the Mississippi River. Using the <u>World Book Encyclopedia</u> and anything else I could find about rivers, I dived into this project. I learned that the Mississippi and its chief tributary, the Missouri, make up one of the longest river systems in the world. Although it may be lovingly referred to as Old Man River, it has caused destruction and pain. I wrote about the flood of 1927 that destroyed homes, barns, and crops—not to mention over 300 people's lives. Stashed with a few yellowed report cards, it remains in the bottom of a drawer. Someone, someday, will have to toss it.

In seventh grade I started confirmation class. A purple book labeled <u>Catechetical Helps</u> by Erwin Kurth had a picture of Martin Luther on page 1. On the next page, B.C. and A.D. were explained, and I felt I had entered the world of knowledge. Although we had daily devotions at home, words like "the law," "the gospel," "prophecy," and "fulfillment" intrigued me.

Thirty-six men wrote sixty-six books over a period of sixteen centuries, and this became the Bible as we know it. And yet it was not a mixture of thoughts but a unified book of God's plan for our salvation. Two years later, on a Sunday in April, I stood straight and spoke softly, but clearly, my chosen, memorized confirmation verse in front of the congregation. "All the rivers run into the sea, yet the sea is not full; unto the place from whence the rivers come, thither they return again." Ecclesiastes 1:7.

Remembering Pastor Steffen's raised eyebrows when I first declared my chosen confirmation verse, I saw the same look on several members of the congregation. My parents, however, smiled. They *knew* me.

A lot of confirmation classmates chose more popular verses, such as John 3:16, "For God loved the world so much that he gave his only Son, so that everyone who believes in him may not die but have eternal life." Or, shorter verses, because they were easy to memorize, like Philippians 4:16, "I can do all things in him who strengthens me." I chose Ecclesiastes 1:7

because, as a young woman, I still had the memory of the little girl in aqua shorts standing near the beginnings of the Mississippi River, the little girl with a great grandmother named Fannie.

The seasons passed. Life grew more complicated. My relationships with my parents and friends changed as I changed and thought about things differently. It happens to all of us.

3

Dressed in a blue-checkered skirt and top with a Jantzen white cardigan over my shoulders and new white tennis shoes, my mother clicked the camera at 7:55 in the morning before I walked the lane to meet the bus. It was tradition: the picture of us on the first day of every school year. However, my brothers were missing. It was the start of my senior year. My older brother Zeke was off to his third year of college in Iowa City, and my brother, Rob, was starting his first year at the local community college. Having Mom and Dad to myself was both a blessing and a bother.

What are you studying? How did your math test go? What's new with your friends? Have you applied for the scholarship? I looked forward to the evenings and weekends either brother showed up.

So, often at night, I would run. It became my escape. I started out running our lane: a quarter mile up, a quarter mile back. A short time later, I ventured to the gravel road and soon was running the section, a four-mile square. I was not afraid of the dark and felt secure and safe in my surroundings. Our neighbors had been the same neighbors for years. Although we were not close, we knew each other. Jim and Nettie Brooks, an older couple, who lived a quarter of a mile east of us, had always rented land from our family. Their house was dark when I ran with the exception of the living room window where a television spilled various lights onto their lawn and cast shadows on the night grass. The Nills, on the next farm, had a lane that dipped and crossed a creek before it ended at a farmhouse completely secluded by a thick grove of trees and brush. Bridget, or Mrs. Nills, was from Germany. It was rumored that she suffered from depression and had tried to commit suicide. Half-way around the section was the Buckle household full of girls and a father others whispered about. My parents never spoke of them except to say that I would not have permission to stay over if they invited me. I didn't understand at the time why the rumors were about *him*. Mrs. Buckle often hung her head and made no eye contact; he was friendly and outgoing. The final household was the Sniderlings, Quakers, who named their four children Faith, Hope, Charity, and Abraham. On the bus, I would just say, "Hi." Their names wouldn't come out. Back then, everyone was named Kathy, Nancy, or Donna.

We were all within walking distance of each other's farms and our families had lived on the same section of land for decades, but we actually knew very little about each other.

Although this was one of many thoughts as I ran, when I looked up and surveyed the wondrous nightly heavens, I was simply amazed and filled with a sense of God's greatness. At these times, I felt God had a plan for me. I could not begin to perceive what it was. Most of the time, I didn't try. I just knew it was out there waiting for me.

There was a song that was popular when I was little. I believe it was Doris Day who sang it. *When I was just a little girl, I asked my mother, what will I be. Will I be pretty? Will I be rich? Here's what she said to me. Que Sera, Sera, whatever will be, will be, the future's not ours to see, Que Sera, Sera...* As a teenager I even sang it; however, I thought it was quite silly. Every girl wants to be pretty. And even though my parents were very frugal, I had never been without what I needed, so being rich didn't seem important. But knowing God had a plan for me was important. I felt pulled toward this in a way I could not explain. It was just there.

My senior year passed quickly with football cheerleading, homecoming, girls' basketball, track, a school play, and falling in love.

Let me tell you about Bill. He'd been smiling at me that special kind of smile I hadn't seen him use on others, and, believe me, I had been watching him. After several weeks of this, he progressed to a *Hi* accompanied by a head nod whenever we met in the halls. Then one day, I felt a presence behind me at my locker. Turning, I saw a grey button-down shirt, nicely pressed, and smelled men's cologne. Bill. Broad shoulders and all--inches from me.

"Aaah... Hi." If a person can stutter saying Hi, this was it. His deep voice was impressive and he stared at me although I don't think he meant to.

"Hi," I answered, and since I was holding my math book, I asked, "Got your algebra done?"

"What's that?" With all the students passing, the halls were filled with chatter and he couldn't hear me. Being extra tall, he sort of dipped his ear toward my face.

"Your algebra assignment. Did you get it done?" I repeated. His eyes were so blue, and I hoped my breath didn't smell like the fish sticks we had had for lunch.

"Oh. Yea. Sure." He nodded and smiled like he hadn't expected me to say anything and was relieved I had.

"Good," I answered because I really didn't know what else to say. We were so used to smiling but not talking. It was awkward, but he started walking beside me on the way to class.

"Can you meet me tonight after the game?" He bent down a bit so I could hear him without everyone else hearing him, too, and his shoulder bumped mine. My heart started doing little flip-flops.

I looked up and saw he was blushing a bit and wanted to make it easier. "Sure. I can meet you. Where?"

"At your locker. After the game." He smiled ever so slightly, and I smiled back. Bill sat in the southeast corner of math class; I sat in the northwest corner of math class, and my eyes were on his broad shoulders that entire period wondering.

After the game, I left the gym and ventured to the classroom section of the building. I don't think anyone was supposed to be there. I climbed the worn, wooden steps causing a creak or two to pierce the great emptiness of a school building at night. Intrigued and a little apprehensive about meeting Bill in total darkness, my heart responded. Taking a deep breath and starting to wonder if he would show up, I was startled when a deep voice came out of the shadows.

"Hi."

I jumped and turned towards the sound.

"Sorry. I didn't mean to scare you." He took hold of one of my hands, and we just stood there not being able to see each other's face.

"That's okay," I whispered thinking *we're really not supposed to be here and we could get into trouble.*

"Can I take you home?" Bill asked.

And, that's how it started. Every Saturday night was Bill and Karen's night. We never missed. We were two high school kids in love. Yet, there was a dilemma, the kind of dilemma that prevented us from having a lasting relationship--at least from my standpoint. I was the first to bring up God. To say that Bill became uneasy is a bit of an understatement.

We had gone to the movie, *Baby, the Rain Must Fall,* with Steve McQueen starring as a parolee who returned to his wife and daughter but who could not stay out of trouble. Steve McQueen's character was definitely mixed-up, but we had no understanding of why he was or why his wife did nothing to set him straight. There were no major confrontations between the two. The characters in the movie and the movie-goers were left confused and even saddened. After all, Steve was a really good-looking guy. We wanted him to be the hero. Something bigger than either of them seemed to be the cause. But, what? Maybe, there were some things in life we were not supposed to understand.

It was the kind of movie that makes one think about a lot of things. Bill and I ended up talking about a lot of stuff that night. Deep stuff, like the purpose of life, why people do the things they do, different kinds of love, and what it means to be in a relationship. And, of course, it led to God. Bill quietly listened to me explain my love of God and what He meant to me, waited a few seconds and, then, with his arms across his chest, stated that he was agnostic. No matter how I tried to convince him to think differently, Bill only smiled and got a twinkle in his eye when I brought God up. He seemed to be entertained by my passion.

As the months passed, I would carefully choose times to bring up our "God discussions" as Bill called them. But, because these debates started causing hard feelings, I stopped. I loved Bill and wanted to be with him; however, my faith in God was serious. I could not have a lasting relationship with someone who did not love God. In addition, our long-term relationship discussions stopped. Bill would bring up the fact that we were both headed for graduation, summer jobs, and college and how it would be difficult to see each other. We were distancing ourselves from one another, but our thinking was different.

Senior Awards Night and graduation passed in a flurry. My family had a small reception at our home with a few relatives, a few neighbors, a couple of teachers and Bill. I left the following Monday for Bethesda Home in Wisconsin, a home for adults and children who were physically and/or mentally disabled. I couldn't tell if Bill was hurt or releived when I told him about my decision to do this, and even though I loved him in a way I had never loved before, I needed to leave home. I knew I had to do something with my life, and it was very possible that Bill was not a part of the picture.

4

It was an old-fashioned hotel with a bespectacled clerk in suspenders standing behind a walnut reception desk. With the smell of diesel lingering, the Greyhound bus headed off as I set my one suitcase down and gave the clerk my name.

"Oh, yes, you'll be here for the summer?" he questioned while chewing on a mottled pencil.

"Yes." I waited for him to look up. He seemed permanently hunched over the registry.

"Working at the home?" he asked as he scribbled notes.

"Yes."

"Okay," he seemed to draw out the "k" part. "Your room number is 212. If you go up these stairs and turn right, it's at the end of the hall." He handed me a three inch key, actually made eye-contact, and pointed to the steps.

"Thank you." I started up a set of dark wooden stairs with dusty corners. At the top, I turned right. Dark-stained, polished, wooden doors with silver numbers on them lined each side of the hallway. The walls were white, but fingerprints and a general dinginess tinted the hallway. With some hesitation, I set my suitcase down, stuck the key in the keyhole and turned it. After a definite click, I opened the door to a room measuring about 12 x 12 feet with a regular sized bed covered with an off-white chenille spread. There was a small closet and a chest of drawers with a mirror attached. The chest was varnished in the same dark color as the doors lining the hallway. I walked to the window covered with an off-white sheer and a pull-shade. I peeked out; the brick building next door filled the entire window. Being used to fields of corn, beans, and pastureland, a general malaise swept through me. I picked up my suitcase, closed the door behind me, and sat on my bed. There was not a sound in the building.

It was three o'clock in the afternoon and I wasn't to report until the next morning. I emptied my suitcase into the drawers and hung a few items in the closet (a dress, a skirt and a blouse) and placed two extra pairs of shoes on the closet floor. I placed a wind-up alarm clock on the dresser and then got down on my knees to slide my gray suitcase under the bed. Still on my knees, I leaned against the bed and placed my elbows on the chenille spread. Holding my face with my hands, I took a deep breath and shuddered. *What* was I doing here?

I remembered months ago viewing the information available at our church about Bethesda Home located in Watertown, Wisconsin. They were looking for youth to be summer workers. The name Bethesda was taken from John 5:2-9 and meant "House of Mercy." The home focused on Christ-centered living for individuals with developmental disabilities. These individuals received support and services while farming, gardening, and tending livestock while also helping to take care of each other. In 1960, the first thrift store started which not only provided jobs to the residents but also provided a source of income for Bethesda and an opportunity for people from the outside world to interact with those from the home.

I reopened my suitcase and pulled the lid flap down. There was a brochure I had incidentally packed. It stated, "As a non-profit organization, Bethesda turns to people like you to help support its ministry. Each year thousands of people volunteer their time at or with the individuals Bethesda serves…." Still kneeling and hearing only an occasional car pass on the main street outside the hotel, I asked myself where these *thousands* were. Feelings of loneliness exacerbated my already saddened disposition.

I thought about my family. My parents and brothers were at home with the usual chores and hard work the farm demanded. I thought about Bill. "What about us?" he had asked when I filled him in on my summer plans, but I didn't have a good answer. We had agreed that we would have to give each other space with college and future plans. Whatever that was. And, of course, there was the "God discussions" history that was on my mind probably much more than on Bill's. I remember walking into the house that night with two separate feelings that seemed to flip-flop, not able to exist together: a feeling of freedom and a feeling of separation. It seemed unfair. *Freedom* was a positive; *separation* had a negative feel to it. I clasped my hands and bowed my head in prayer. Before any words came, one of my confirmation verses did. "Blessed is the man who trusts in the Lord, whose trust is the Lord. He is like a tree planted by water…"

A few tears dribbled on my tightly folded hands as I asked God to forgive me, to guide me, and to help me trust Him in all things. I took a deep breath, stood, said Amen, grabbed my purse and three-inch door key, and took the steps down to the lobby. Looking around, I spotted a large wall map of Watertown, Wisconsin, with facts about the state and interesting trivia. I learned that Wisconsin was an Indian word with several possible meanings including "gathering of the waters."

With a prayer of thanks on my lips, I opened the hotel door and stepped out into the heat of a June day. I walked up the street noting a hardware store, a jewelry store, a women's clothing store, and Maid-Rite Café. Remembering that I had not eaten since leaving home that morning, I pushed the glass door open and a bell attached tinkled my presence. The waitress looked up from cleaning a large coffee pot.

"Can I help you?"

She was probably my age. This was most likely her summer job.

"Can I help you?" She asked again somewhat impatiently.

"Yes, a Maid-Rite, please, with pickles."

"Something to drink?"

"Water's fine," I answered noting her name tag, Teresa.

I sat down at a counter stool and picked up the paper. The heading read: "Government of the People, By the People and For the People." I skimmed an article about the 1965 Voting Rights Act which prohibited states from discriminatory practices such as poll taxes and literacy tests intended to bar Blacks from the voting booths. Above the news heading was a photo of a black lady smiling while displaying her certificate of eligibility to vote. Another article read "Vietnam: Another World." Flipping to the entertainment/social section, I noted a picture of the Supremes with an article about Motown Records. A small article about Julie Nixon and David Eisenhower's romance filled a corner spot, and, on another page, an advertisement proclaimed that the circus was coming to town. I felt disconnected in a strange town with so much happening in the world, but I was not a part of any of it.

Teresa plunked the Maid Rite on the counter in front of me and set a napkin and fork beside the plate.

"Anything else?" She seemed eager to be elsewhere.

"Water, please." I watched as she turned and filled a water glass. I wanted to ask if she had just graduated, if she lived in Watertown, if she had friends, and, yet, I had no right. I only smiled and thanked her as she placed the glass in front of me.

The sandwich was huge. Using a fork, I cut it in half as an orangish goo dribbled onto the plate. After finishing every last crumb, I checked my watch and noted that it was 5 p.m. I left a tip, walked out of the already empty café, and ventured back to the hotel. Remembering the stationery Mom had persuaded me to pack, I located a pen in the bottom of my purse and started writing.

Dear Mom and Dad,

The bus trip went fine. I slept part of the way but mostly took in the scenery and visited with a lady sitting next to me. She was a grandma going to help her daughter who was having her second child. She was very excited and had pictures to share.

I checked in. It's a small room with a window but no scenery. (A brick wall—ugh!) I walked a ways, bought a sandwich and will get some letters written. Everything is really quiet.

I'll write later this week. I start tomorrow. Hope it goes ok.

Love,

Karen

I sealed it and licked a stamp from a sheet my mom had sent. Remembering there was a postal box outside the hotel, I left my room and headed down the hall when I heard a commotion in the lobby. Two guys and three girls, about my age, were laughing. They all had luggage, and I heard "Bethesda" once or twice while the somewhat befuddled clerk was doing over-time on the pencil. In spite of the new group, who all apparently knew each other, I felt more alone than ever. With only a glance, they passed me on the steps as they headed to their respective rooms.

Stepping outside, the sun hot and oppressive, feeling sorry for myself, I again, questioned my decision about coming. Why did I often feel so alone, so alienated, so separated in new situations? Was this a human condition? If so, why wasn't it obvious in others? For example, the others who had just arrived? My mother recognized this tendency of mine early. "You're always questioning, Karen, wondering, and asking why." I could hear her voice inside my head and I had to smile as I remembered her reminding me that Jesus asked his disciples, "Can anxious thought add a single day to your life?" And, so, I realized that if I were to fit in, I would have to walk back into the hotel, walk up the steps, and introduce myself. I dropped the letter into the post office box and headed inside away from the afternoon heat.

One. Two. Three. Four. I counted the steps. Turn right. I stopped at an open door and saw three girls sitting on the bed fanning their faces.

"Hi. I'm Karen. I checked in earlier. I overheard you talking. You'll be volunteering at Bethesda?"

They all nodded. One of them stood up.

"I'm Becki, this is Lavonne, and this is Sherri. We're trying to decide about rooms. None of us really wants to room alone. We can't decide…"

Without a lot of thought, I interrupted, "One of you could room with me. I'm by myself."

They all looked at me. I couldn't tell if they were close friends or not. They would either want to stay together or they wouldn't care.

Sherri stood up and asked, "Where's your room? If it's okay with you, you have a roommate."

"Great," I smiled at her.

We headed down the hall and stopped at the boys' room. Sherri introduced me to Will and Tom. They were trying to open a window and complaining about the heat. Before the day was over, we had taken a walk together, grabbed snacks at a local grocery and made predictions about what volunteer work would be like at Bethesda. Deciding we had already had a long day and the next day would be even longer, we separated around ten p.m. and tried to get some sleep.

· · · · · · · · · · · · · · · · · ·

I had been given a diary with key and lock for my tenth birthday and had good intentions as a young girl to write my life story one day at a time. A girl with long brown hair in a nice red sweater, pencil in hand, was pictured on the cover. I had lost the key over the years and written intermittently. It had been a last-minute addition to my suitcase.

Day 1

My first day at Bethesda. We had a tour, met some of the residents and employees. Skeptical looks from both sides. I can tell these few weeks are going to be something.

Day 8

I love it here. God created these people; they're wonderful. Did general support jobs. It's boring work, but I'm learning about people. Wrote Mom and Dad.

Day 11

Stayed up in LaVonne and Becky's room along with Will, Tom, and Sherri. Talked until 12:30. Not looking forward to tomorrow. Tired. Wondering what Bill is doing.

Day 13

Worked in general supply. Had picnic supper with residents. Went for pizza later with the group. Talked till 2 a.m. Thought about writing Bill. What would I say? It all felt so funny when I left; he was such a big part of my life.

Day 16

Took group of residents to Wisconsin Dells. One became too attached, wanting to hold hands. Also picnicked. Some other vacationers looked at me as if, "Are you one of them?" Is this how the residents feel? Or, don't they know?

Day 20

Found out today we have to put on a program for everyone before we leave. We are all getting worn out. The food is strange. There is always this cheese-whiz with raisins mixture they serve…. Missing Mom and Dad. Missing Bill.

Our volunteer group had become close knit. We shared stories of our families, laughed at each other's jokes, and discussed our daily experiences in our work with adults with developmental disabilities. But they were not family and this was not home.

After a couple of weeks, I received two letters: one from my mom and one from Bill. Mom wrote about walking beans and doing some canning, and filled me in on neighborhood gossip. The letter from Bill was a bit of a surprise. We hadn't talked about keeping in touch. I missed him, yet *I* had not written. Although I was not romantically interested in either Will or Tom from our volunteer group, I was having fun hanging out and not having to think about being loyal to someone else.

That particular night, we were planning on going as a group to the movie theater in a nearby town. We were all excited about this venture: time away from Bethesda! I pulled my suitcase out from underneath the bed, pulled open the side sash and stuck the unopened letter from Bill inside.

The following days seemed to fade along with summer. Working side by side with the residents, we sorted clothing in the Thrift Store, went for walks, ate with them, and were responsible for entertainment on Saturday nights. It was rewarding, challenging, and exhausting. I began to understand persons with disabilities in a different way. Like each of us, they had no choice as to their birth circumstances. They did not choose to be born deformed or mentally deficient. Yet, when the general public came into the Thrift Shop, I noted that the adults we worked with were sometimes treated with disdain as if the physical or mental deficiencies were a result of some choice they had personally made. Most of the residents were not aware that some viewed them offensively. They found pure joy in the flight of a bird, a certain color, or a spontaneous smile.

The last night we were in Watertown, our volunteer group drove into Milwaukee. Everyone was excited about going home but we started to sense that something would be missing in all of our lives. We would miss each other, we would miss some of the residents, and we realized that we were forever changed because of this mission. I was okay with going home. I was in a sense relieved this part of my summer was over.

Sitting in the hotel lobby I uncomfortably waited for the Greyhound bus to arrive. Dressed in shorts, a crop top, and white tennis shoes, my legs stuck to the wooden chair as I pushed my bangs off a damp forehead. I had packed the previous night after returning from Milwaukee and did not sleep well. The volunteer group had met earlier to say our goodbyes and exchange addresses. The others had left, and I was alone feeling much the same way I did when I had first arrived.

I heard the bus shift gears outside, and as I stood up realized I had a slight headache. Need more sleep, I told myself. The driver picked up my suitcase, and I boarded the bus. I found a seat halfway back by a window and settled in. In my carry-on bag, I had money, a magazine, quickly written goodbye notes from the other volunteers, and the unopened letter from Bill. I stared out the window at passers-by and fell into a deep sleep as the bus left the hotel.

I dreamed about rivers. I'm sure we crossed several during the trip although I do not specifically remember any. M I S S I S S I P P I chants took up space in my mind as I felt the cooling spray from a waterfall. My new-found friends from my summer experience were splashing each other in the stream. In my dream, I turned to watch and wonder where the water continued its path around a bend. This is when I saw him. A young man standing in the stream looking towards me with arms out-stretched. Walking the sandy bank, my feet sinking in to my ankles, I approached this person, but he kept drifting farther downstream as if he were caught up in the current. He was not afraid. Just drifting—with arms outstretched. Bill?

It was late when I finally arrived home to the farm that night. After answering a few quick questions from my parents and brothers, I took a shower and wearily climbed the stairs to slip under sheets just a little cooler than the night air. With the window wide open by my bedside, I listened to hogs banging the metal lids on their feeders. Did they eat all night? They soon quieted, and the sound of crickets filled the night air. A gentle breeze washed through the room. Although my world could not have felt safer or more secure, I had a general apprehension I could not explain. The peculiar dream on my bus ride home kept playing inside my head like a determined re-run until I forced myself to think of something, anything else. Making a mental list of things I needed to do the next day, I stared through the tree's darkened branches and studied the blinking of stars in a very black sky.

5

"What does Johnson think he's doing?" I could hear my father ask someone, anyone from the breakfast table. Awakened by his uncharacteristically loud voice, I put my feet on the floor, sat up, and stretched. Home. A good feeling.

"It's a mess! Our young ones are killed, wounded or permanently disabled. For what?" I heard a newspaper being folded and mom murmuring quietly, perhaps in an attempt to settle my father.

I got up and quietly descended the steps. What were they talking about? I heard the back door slam and dishes being placed in the sink.

"Mom, what's wrong with Dad?" I asked as I entered the kitchen.

"Oh, good morning, honey. So nice to have you home."

"What is it? What's wrong with Dad? Why is he so angry? Who's being killed?" I persisted.

"Oh, well, your dad. He's against the war in Vietnam. The neighbor kid, you remember Danny, he's being sent. Your father is upset about it."

I picked up the newspaper and read bits and pieces. In 1957, Communist forces began to attack villages in South Vietnam which developed into the Vietnam War. Many Vietnamese were forced from their homes to refugee camps. Thousands were being killed. I'm sure my dad was worried about his very own sons having to fight a war he didn't believe in. I viewed the map of Vietnam in the paper noting the Mekong River and felt a strange pull. *The letter.* Bill's letter. I got up, dropped the newspaper on the floor, and took the steps two at a time to my bedroom. Opening my unpacked suitcase, I rifled through it and then remembered I had stashed it in my carry-on bag. I turned it upside down and emptied the contents. There it was. I had not been interested in opening it before, but now, I was almost afraid to open it. I slid my fingernail under a loose edge and clumsily ripped it open.

Dear Karen,

Hope you don't mind. Got your address from your Mom. Well, I went and did it. Signed up with the Marines. College will have to wait. Can't really explain why I did it, and my folks don't understand either.

I just wanted to let you know. Didn't want you to hear it from someone else. I leave in a month. Maybe I'll see you when you get home.
You know I love you,
Bill

With tears in my eyes I walked to my dresser and laid down the letter. I looked into the mirror and saw a young woman with long, uncombed brown hair; dark brown eyes outlined with thick lashes, and I looked somewhat thin. What was I thinking? How could I be so self-centered as to get a letter and, then, stash it unread because its contents just might interfere with my summer life. There was a war going on and I had chosen to be oblivious.

Closing the door to my room, I lay on my bed with fists clenched. Bill and Vietnam; coming home after spending a summer with adults with developmental disabilities and seeing the world differently; breaking connections with the other volunteers; coming back home to a loving family. It was everything and yet nothing in particular. I unpacked my suitcase and attempted to organize my room. I needed time for the redness to disappear from my eyes.

I carried my dirty laundry downstairs and then picked up the phone. Bill's number. I knew it by heart.

"Hello," a voice answered. I recognized it as Bill's mom.

"Evelyn, how are you? This is Karen. Is Bill there?"

"Oh. Hi. Karen. Actually, Bill is not here. He just left. Yesterday. For basic training. He had hoped to hear from you." She spoke haltingly. "Sorry you missed him."

"I'm so sorry. I didn't know." I hung up without saying good bye.

That night I ran the section—four miles. I was out of shape; I had not been running most of the summer. Tired and out of breath, I plopped down in a soft spot in the ditch at the end of our driveway and looked up at the heavens. The moon appeared as a banana hung in the night sky. Stars and planets did their twinkling thing. God's creation. Awesome. He created all this and yet he cares for me. I asked God to forgive me for my self-centeredness and a whole bunch of other things. I prayed that he would keep Bill safe and that the Vietnam War would end soon.

6

"**D**on't forget your address book," Mom yelled up the stairs. "We expect a letter now and then."

I smiled. Of course I would write my parents. I finished packing one suitcase with clothes for college/nursing school, locked it up and pulled another empty one out of my closet. Trying to decide what to pack next, I tackled a stack of papers on my dresser. One was a letter from Jolene Norby, director of nursing, at the school I would be attending.

"Dear Karen," it read. "The health industry is facing a critical shortage of qualified personnel. Across the country, registered nurses, along with many other professionals from the health field are in demand." The director closed with a, "We look forward to meeting you!"

On top of the paper stack, I plopped William Golding's *Lord of the Flies*—required reading for freshmen students to be used during orientation discussions. Golding attempted to trace the defects of civilization back to the defects of human nature. In the summer heat, I became acquainted with Ralph, Piggy, Jack, Simon and a band of boys abandoned on an uninhabited island with no adult supervision. Having grown up on a farm in the Midwest and being somewhat introspective, I spent a little time thinking about neighbors, friends, and family members and why they did what they did. However, thinking about the implications of human nature on society or vice versa was beyond me. I realized my college learning experiences would go further than nurse's training.

I was leaving in a couple of days, and both my brothers were moving back to their respective colleges the following week. My parents would have a busy few days. I teased them about getting lonely in the coming months. With the farm work and the summer heat, they smiled weakly and agreed—too tired to tease back.

I had called Evelyn, again, and gotten Bill's address. He would be home after basic training, but I would be gone. Making up a story about how I had gotten the letter late while in Wisconsin, how they must have lost it at the hotel kind-of-thing, I wrote Bill a letter of apology for not responding to his first letter sooner. I sent my school address, told him I was thinking of him, and asked him to write. I closed by telling him that he was in my prayers.

The next few weeks were a flurry of orientation, setting up schedules, adjusting to dorm life and roommates, and starting classes. My courses were Health and Nursing Assessment, Biology, Chemistry, and Introduction to the Profession of Nursing. Because I would need a C or better to continue with each semester's classes, I dug in fervently with assignments. I requested to sit in the front of my classes, asked questions, and took notes. Even though Bill and I had separated, I knew some of my passion was the result of his going into the service. It was no longer a high school world. I could only imagine some of the horrendous experiences he might experience. The least I could do was to focus on my studies.

Letters came. From home. From Bill. Even a letter or two from my volunteer friends from Bethesda. Although I was relieved Bill wrote, I did not look forward to his letters. He had not talked about joining the service while we dated, and I didn't understand his decision to do so. Was it the impending draft? Was it simply not knowing what he wanted to do with his life?

I chose not to date anyone. It just didn't seem right. And, it had to do with the decision *he* made. Because of this there were many times I spent by myself, especially on the weekends. I would often go to The Falls Park located at the edge of town. There was a picnic area, a walk-over bridge, lots of grass and trees and, of course the falls, itself. Sitting at the falls' edge, feeling the spray as the water dashed against the rocks, I would often think of my favorite Bible verse learned many years ago from Ecclesiastes, "All the rivers run into the sea; yet the sea is not full; unto the place from whence the rivers come, theither, they return again."

I prayed that Bill would remain strong and protected during basic training and later in the war zones of Vietnam and that he would return safely to his family and friends. I prayed that I would be open to God's plan for my life. I also prayed ardently that Bill would come to love the Lord and accept Him as the Savior for his life. As I watched the water splash and bounce against the huge rocks, I thought about the fact that although rivers are useful to people, they are also potentially dangerous- -like a person. Rivers carry huge quantities of sediment which affects the surrounding landscape. Its power can be so great that it can erode the land

and change its shape--like a person. Flowing water, harnessed, is an endless source of energy. Where would my energies lead me?

The weeks passed. Lectures, homework, exams, time spent on a hospital ward mostly shadowing. I went home for a much needed break over Thanksgiving weekend. Everything and yet nothing was the same. "You can never go home again." Whoever said it—now, it had a meaning for me. Because I had changed, because my parents lifestyle had changed due to the empty-nest situation, because my brothers were learning and experiencing life as never before, our home as we once knew it was not the same.

Uncle Art and Aunt Marion were there with some of my cousins. There was turkey, dressing, mashed potatoes, sweet potatoes, gravy, onion casserole, cranberries, and two kinds of pie. I wondered what Bill was eating. Talk about the harvest—mostly completed—and what the *Farmer's Almanac* predicted for winter weather filled the dining room. Mom talked to me about Christmas plans and would I give her a list?

Time passed: holiday parties, winter storms, thawing snow, final exams, the arrival of spring. With one year of college successfully completed, I returned home to help with summer work. It was a long, tedious summer as many high school friends whom I might have connected with had jobs elsewhere. Letters from the Bethesda experience had stopped and even Bill's letters had dwindled. I wondered if he was interested in someone else or just didn't have time to write. I read a lot, did some sewing, helped with the usual farmwork, and was relieved when August showed up and I packed for a second school year.

7

Starting a second year of college was a little less stressful than being a freshman. No orientation, no *Lord of the Flies*, no learning one's way around the campus. Another Thanksgiving with the usual family food favorites and aunts, uncles and cousins seated around our large dining room table arrived like clockwork. With leftovers carefully divided, Mom and Dad sent my brothers and me back to school with an appeal for another Christmas list.

While the outside world primped for Christmas, I spent hours at the library cramming for tests and completing papers—coffee logged and weary. After final exams and before heading home, I hastily chose a few family gifts and one for Bill. He had written that he would be home and could he see me?

Looking picture perfect, a light dusting of snow blanketed the ground and whitened the family farm. As I looked up into our yard light, the snow continued to sift down in big butterfly flakes. I wrapped my unbuttoned navy coat across my chest and held tightly in an attempt to calm myself and stay warm. I was a little excited and slightly anxious.

I was dressed in a black wool skirt and white turtle-neck sweater—not too dressy, not too casual. I hadn't seen Bill since high school graduation. A year and one half had passed. Words like Khe Sanh, la Drang, A Shau, Saigon, Danang, Quang Tri, Can Tho, and An Loc from his letters came from a world I could only imagine. He was in a place I did not want him to be. I came to understand that the sights, sounds, and even smells of Vietnam would be forever imprinted in his mind. I ached for him. I prayed for him. And, then, I went back to my own work. I tried not to watch the news or even read the paper about the war. America was so divided over Vietnam, yet young men were being trained, sent overseas, and dying. It seemed so pointless.

We talked briefly on the phone after his arrival back to the states. It was a simple, uncomfortable conversation. I knew he would call; he had written that he would.

"Karen?" His voice was raspier than I had remembered. Was he nervous?

"Yes, it's me. Hi."

"Hi," he returned, and I was immediately taken back to high school where Bill had first said *hi* to me. I remembered the gray-starched shirt, his blue eyes, the smell of cologne, his broad shoulders. The old feelings returned without my permission and sent tingling sensations up my spine and goose bumps down my arms. With that call, I yearned to reconnect and make sure he was okay, and yet I was apprehensive. What were his feelings? Did I even understand my own? We had become pen-pals of sorts always safely signing our letters, *Just me.*

As I heard the gravel crunch under his car tires on our lane, I looked up again at the yard light to watch the snowflakes as they mingled and fell and mumbled a small prayer. "God help me; God help us."

Bill pulled up behind our garage and got out of the car. He seemed taller and stronger, and I sensed aggressiveness in his walk. After a quick hug and a "Hi, how are you," I brought him into the house to see my parents. My mom offered food; my dad discussed the weather. Harmless conversation, thank goodness, especially considering my dad's views on the war.

Miracle on 34th Street was showing in town, but we decided to hang out with old friends. The ride into town was filled with safe questions, quietly asked, as if we were both afraid of each other. How is college? Was basic training hard? What do you do at the hospital? We were both being cautious in a gentle way.

A group of former high school friends gathered. Not knowing whether we were still "kids" or how to act into an adult world, we were somewhat guarded. A few memories were shared. *Remember Mr. Chase when he messed up the science experiment? Remember the cinnamon rolls with chili, a favorite, for school lunch?* Although not specifically talked about, the war was on everyone's mind, especially the guys. Bill was one of two servicemen there; the rest were in college or the work world. I understood America was divided over the war, and I could sense it even here. These college guys had to realize, that in all reality, they might end up serving in this war, even if not by choice.

The ride home was quiet. Bill and I had spent a lot of time together in high school; we were not strangers. And, yet, the phrase, *you can never go home again,* came to my mind, again. The world had changed; we had changed; our relationship had changed. Because of all of this, I didn't know how the evening would end. How do you say goodbye? I knew there was a possibility I would never see him again. Men were dying in Vietnam. The thought sickened me. Bill's thoughts, however, were somewhere else.

He put the car in park, placed his arm around me and nuzzled my neck with a tender kiss. It felt good to be close to him.

"Karen, I've been thinking...."

"Yes," I answered, starting to relax.

"Let's get married."

"What?" I almost jumped out of his arms.

"Let's get married," he repeated but with less enthusiasm.

"You're not joking, are you?" I looked into his eyes.

"No. I'm not." He took a deep breath and I immediately knew the courage it had taken to ask.

"We can't," I stammered, pulling away.

"Why can't we?" He persisted.

"I'm in college. You're overseas." I couldn't say *Vietnam.*

"We're right in the middle of everything," I continued. "Besides that...," and I paused. There was no way to get the words right. "I don't know where we are—you and me. I don't understand it." I couldn't say, "You don't believe in God."

I immediately noted the hurt in his eyes, but he covered it quickly.

"I know. It was just a passing thought." And then he laughed. And I laughed, too. But the laughter was empty, and so were my insides. He wanted something I couldn't give him. He wanted some hope to carry with him when he returned to the war zone. I felt as if I had betrayed him; he had been my high school sweetheart in a world we no longer lived in.

In a gentlemanly fashion, he got out of the car, came around to my side, and opened the door. I was still astonished and bewildered. I took his hand in mind as we walked to the door. At the door, he took hold of my other hand, turning me to face him.

"Karen, I want to share something with you. I can't do it now, but I'll write you about it." I didn't know how to respond, so I said nothing. He went on, "Can I still write?" And, with this he smiled and I smiled back.

"Of course."

I kissed him gently on the cheek as he looked at me in a way he never had with those deep, blue eyes, squeezed my hands, turned, and left.

I stood staring at his back. With contrasting snowflakes softly landing in his brown hair and across his shoulders, I remembered the gift. A brown, v-neck, pullover, XLT, still under our family tree. I wouldn't be able to give it to him. Under the circumstances, it was out of place, inappropriate. Too personal and not personal at all.

He didn't look up when he got in his car. He backed out of the driveway, then turned and looked at me and gave a slight wave with his hand. I listened to the sound of snow beneath his tires as he slowly drove down our lane. Turning to look at his footsteps in the snow and with tears streaming down my face, I watched the snowflakes, bit by bit, erase them. I never saw him again.

Four weeks later, after returning to school, Mom called with the news. Bill. Dead. Vietnam. Funeral. She would come and pick me up.

I attended the memorial service, but I do not remember much. I read the funeral pamphlet, *In Memory of…, Son of…. Born….Died…. Services At…. Officiating…. Interment… Casket Bearers…. The Lord is my Shepherd; I shall not want…. And I will dwell in the house of the Lord forever.*

I will dwell in the house of the Lord forever? Bill's family was agnostic. I studied Bill's family as they filed into the funeral home to their assigned chairs and looked for an explanation as if it could be found in their demeanor. The fact that the service was led by a pastor should have been some kind of sign.

He introduced himself as Pastor Hoppwell and welcomed both family and friends before he went on to state that Bill had a particular Bible verse he had wanted at this service. I looked at my mother, seated beside me, my hand in both of hers. Maybe she knew something.

For I am sure that neither death, nor life, nor angels, nor principalities, nor things present, nor things to come, nor powers, nor height, nor death, nor anything else in all creation, will be able to separate us from the love of God in Christ Jesus our Lord. Romans 8:38, 39

Two of his friends spoke, and the minister offered consoling words; however, I could not concentrate. Relief, confusion, grief smothered me like a heavy blanket until I felt ill. Mom asked if I needed to leave, get some air. I took a deep breath, sat up straight, shook my head knowing I needed to be there for Bill's family.

After the service, Bill's mom approached me.

"Karen, thanks for coming," Evelyn told me. Her face was drawn, her coloring was poor. She looked awful. I could not imagine the depths of her loss.

"Evelyn, I'm so sorry," I murmured hugging her tightly.

As she hugged me back she spoke. "I need to let you know that Bill and his father and I had a long discussion before he returned to Vietnam. I can't remember all the details, but he became a Christian. He said it was because of you. He wanted to tell you when he was home, but didn't think the timing was right."

Speechless, I cried uncontrollably as Evelyn continued to hold me.

"I needed to let you know. He would want you to know." And, with this, she released me, went on to others, accepting their condolences, staying strong in an impossible circumstance.

8

My parents returned me to school with *are-you-going-to-be-ok?* between every other question and phrase. The rest of the year passed; my grades dropped. It was a period of concentrated sadness. Experiencing little joy or satisfaction, my life was empty. Black and white. I moved myself to the back of the room in my classes and caught myself daydreaming, but later had no recollection of what I was thinking. And, at unexpected times, I experienced intense feelings of guilt.

My parents called often. I responded with "yeses" and "nos," and tried to cut the conversation short. I had nothing to say. One day, my college advisor called me in to discuss my grades. She was concerned. Catching me at a weak moment, I started sobbing in her office and telling her my recent life history. Everything was so wrong. But, from that very low point, and with her gracious help, I was able to begin to turn things around.

A Christian, she shared with me Romans 8:28.

Moreover we know that to those who love God, who are called according to his plan, everything that happens fits into a pattern for good.

It was spring, and I found myself venturing back to The Falls Park at the edge of town and rethinking the river analogy. *Rivers carry huge quantities of sediment which affects the surrounding landscape.* I had been carrying a huge burden the last few months, and it was affecting the world around me—my classes, my roommates, my family. *Its power can be so great, that it can erode the land and change its shape.* I did not want my depressed state to be the power that influenced my life. *Flowing water, harnessed, is an endless source of energy.* I had stagnated. I knew I needed to reconnect with God. It would take time. When the depression overwhelmed me, and it continued to do so at unpredictable times, I would repeat my confirmation Bible verse and say a quick prayer asking God for forgiveness and thanking him for his grace in time of need.

Bill was gone. I would never see him again. I couldn't understand it--why it had to end the way it did. Could I have done anything to prevent this? The wonder in all of this, however, was that Bill had accepted Christ before he died. I had to praise God for this. Why didn't Bill tell me? Did he think I would think he had become a Christian so that I would marry him? There were no answers to any of these questions. I was heart-broken, and I could not rid myself of the guilt.

The spring semester ended. My grades were nothing to write home about, but I knew they would get better. That summer I took a job at the hospital as a nurse's aid, lived in the dorm, and took a summer class, Introduction to Art. I could get an elective credit for it, and I convinced myself that the change of pace would be good. I was not artistic in the least. An additional bonus came from taking the class: meeting Margo.

Introduction to Art was a two credit hour elective class. I took it because it fit with my work schedule and because I wanted to think about something else besides health care. I learned that, in a large sense, art is a skill in making or doing. We covered a gamut of subjects including carving, ceramics, engraving, photography, sculpture, and painting. I was introduced to styles of art, such as, Arabesque, Baroque, Surrealism, Realism and Romanticism. Although I had little natural talent, I learned an appreciation for the aesthetic experience such as a masterpiece painting or classical music. *Composition, design, perspective,* and *style* were words that took on a new meaning. After visiting a museum or gallery and losing all track of time because of my concentrated attention, I would leave somehow refreshed, uplifted, and introspective. The guilt feelings were buried temporarily.

I met Margo on day one. She sat beside me. We both had grown up on farms in the Midwest and had attended small high schools. She was kind, considerate and wanted to be an art teacher. She liked to paint; I liked to write poetry. We decided that someday we would publish a book--a book of poems written by me and illustrated by her. We often grabbed a quick lunch in the college cafeteria before I ran off to work at the hospital and she was off to work at a daycare center. On weekends, she'd pick me up and we would enjoy a good meal spending more money than we could afford at a really nice restaurant. And we talked. We knew everything about each other in a few short weeks. Margo listened sympathetically and cried with me when I spilled my feelings about Bill and all the unanswered questions. She had a brother, Martin, serving in Vietnam. We could be quiet together or both chatter at the same time and be at ease. I told her about the M I S S I S S I P P I chant and my confirmation verse. She couldn't remember hers, but she did express that she believed in Jesus Christ as her Savior. To this day, whenever I visit an art museum I think of Margo.

Later that year, my grieving took an angry note. I wrote a poem that was published in the student anthology titled "Leaves Were Falling Like Rain." I had originally written it for Margo. Her boyfriend, after a two year relationship, had broken up with her. With empathy I wrote the poem. It was not uplifting in the least. In fact, it was depressing. I typed it on crisp paper with my Smith Corona being careful not to make any errors and presented it to her as I said, "I'm so sorry."

Leaves were falling like rain,
Trees becoming barren,
When he took my life from me.
He took it
Not to keep
But to cast aside
For the birds to nibble on during the cold months.
Winter protected me with a cold blanket of snow,
And thus, I spent my first Christmas
In hibernation
Away from the world of joy and celebration.
I was neither content nor satisfied,
But I was
Numb to the World,
And so nothing really mattered.
I can't remember, but
Spring must have come and gone,
Because leaves are still falling like rain.
Or are they tears?

Margo unfolded the sheet I had presented to her and read it carefully. As she read it, heaviness filled me. I had written the poem for Margo, but realized it was about me. I was angry for Bill dying, angry that he had not told me he was a Christian. Bill was dead. But, I was lost. It was a pathetically sad poem—presenting a hopeless loss. Although our circumstances were different, Margo and I shared a burden. In the meantime, Margo had been secretly working on a project—a painting of a little girl dressed in aqua shorts standing knee-deep in a stream, a smile on her face.

Margo and I ended up as roommates our senior year. She was off to her art and education classes; I was off to the hospital or a lecture. Our class of nursing students had started our freshmen year by practicing on each other: taking temperatures, blood pressure, and pulse rates. Giving injections to oranges, and, then, with sterile water to each other was somewhat more challenging. My senior year was spent caring for newborns, the elderly, veterans at the VA hospital and helping with family care in a clinic. The Vietnam War continued. Although we set off for parties on the weekends in our checkered bell-bottoms and hoop earrings with smiles and giggles with a group of friends, inwardly we shared the agony of the war. Bill was dead because of Vietnam. Margo had a brother alive and serving in Vietnam. She would share her letters with me, but we discussed it very little. She did not like to think of what her brother might be going through. I did not want to think about what Bill had gone through. We cared deeply and, yet, we were helpless to care in a greater sense.

May and graduation came. It was 1969. Both of our parents came, and we had a small reception in the house we lived in. My brothers were both there. Rob was farming with my parents and came with them. Zeke had a job as an accountant and took a half day off to come. I was presented with a nursing cap representing the hospital/school I had graduated from and a diploma. I saw pride in all of their eyes. Margo's brother was home on leave and came with her parents. Margo had shared her letters from Martin, but I had never been able to picture him. His letters had always seemed void of emotion, short and perfunctory as if the writer had been completing a homework assignment.

There were gifts and cards. I presented Margo with a leather bound journal to encourage her to develop writing skills. She surprised me with her painting. I hugged her and told her I would keep it forever. Painted in bright colors, it was titled, "All Rivers Run Into the Sea." A dark colored tree stood like an umbrella over a little girl in aqua colored shorts knee deep in a stream. Margo knew of my fascination with streams, lakes, and rivers; I was delighted with the gift.

9

In spite of final exams, graduation, the Vietnam War, wanting to get jobs, we had other needs. LOVE. We were a generation of youth who believed in the value of freedom, love, peace, and community. In 1967, San Francisco's Golden Gate Park became the birthplace of the hippies or flower children. Although we wore hippie garb and sang along with the Supremes as they belted out "Baby Love," "Stop in the Name of Love," and "Where Did Our Love Go," we were conservative mid-western college students who had never attended a love-in or an out door weekend concert.

We hung out at the local bars and coffee houses occasionally and loved to have fun. But, we all dreamed of the day when we would meet our knight in shining armor, the person we would share the rest of our life with, our best friend, someone to laugh and cry with, someone who understood our fears, someone who cared about our dreams, and the someone who made us feel good about ourselves. Those were not my thoughts, however, when I fell in love with Martin. Margo never intended for it to happen. I never intended for it to happen.

When I first saw him at my graduation reception, I was smitten. I can't think of a better word. I turned around after hugging my parents and there he was. Staring at me. He was tall, broad shouldered, and wore a dark uniform. He was studying me, and I had to look away. As I felt my face grow warm, Margo touched my arm and said, "Karen, meet Martin."

"Hi." I extended my hand for him to shake and realized my armpits were sticky. He did not resemble Margo at all.

"Karen, nice to meet you. Margo's written about you." He looked at me with dark eyes as he continued to hold my hand in both of his. I was uncomfortable, and the chemistry between us was tangible.

Margo's attention was diverted by a friend as Martin continued to hold my hand.

"Well. Nice to meet you." Feeling faint, I looked away and pulled my hand out of both of his large hands. "I'll talk to you later," I murmured as I thought *what a stupid thing to say.*

Speechless, I headed for the red punch bowl wishing he would not be following while also wishing he would. I gulped a half glass. I *wanted* to go back and look into his eyes and feel the warmth of his hands on mine. Instead I headed for the bathroom to splash cool water on my face. Looking into the mirror I noted that my pupils were dilated and my face was flush. I took a deep breath, told myself to grow up, and headed back to the reception.

While visiting with friends who had stopped, I noted that Martin was alone and looking out our picture window with his hands folded behind his back. They were a deep tan as was his neck. His hair was dark and very curly with a strip of gray behind one ear. I thought it unusual for one so young. What must it be like to look out at green grass, flowers, and a sky filled with cotton-puff clouds while listening to harmless chatter and laughter when he had come from a combat zone? He looked out of place. I watched him as a group of my friends approached him—also fascinated. He turned and seemed somewhat entertained by their banter. He smiled. But not really.

I approached the group, stood at the edge and listened.

"What time did you say the barbeque was?....I'm wearing....She looked so fat in that .....Can you believe.....When did you say you were going home?.....I can hardly wait......I applied....." And, on and on.

Throughout their conversations to impress him, his eyes followed me. And, mine were on him.

Instead of the barbeque or other receptions, I had dinner that night with Martin. With college graduation complete, many students were headed home, starting vacations or off to that first real job. Others were celebrating at private parties. The bistro was virtually empty. Quiet. Romantic. The feeling that exists when two people first meet and chemistry exists was pervasive. Like quiet fire-works, tangible and exquisite, I wanted to stick a measure of it in my purse and take it home. I felt a heightened sensitivity to my surroundings, yet my focus was totally on Martin. We talked, but not a lot. We simply were two people together in a moment of time.

He took me back to my college residence. As I took the step and turned to say good night, he enfolded me in his arms and kissed me tenderly and extensively. I wanted to melt inside his embrace and exist there forever.

I watched him leave, being too limp to open the door and walk inside. It had been a marvelous night. He didn't call the next day, or the next. A week later, I learned through Margo, inadvertently, as she was unaware of my date with Martin, that he had returned to his camp base somewhere in California. No one knew about my feelings for Martin; I was beginning to wonder if Martin even knew. I remembered how in grade school we would write notes to each other to find out who liked whom. *Dear Martin, Do you like me? Check yes or no? Karen.* My feelings seemed childish, but I could not make them go away.

As time passed, I kept thinking back to that night trying to recall every detail: the way he touched me, his warm breath on my cheek, his total embrace, his cologne. It took my breath away to think of it; that is how powerful my feelings were. I still wonder what the magnetism was, the draw on that particular night.

I did not write. How could I write a person who had spent one evening looking lovingly into my eyes, kissing me passionately and, then, left without saying "Goodbye, write me," or "I'll call." I was forced to question my deepest, hidden feelings which included my on-going grief and anger over Bill's death.

The weeks passed. Margo accepted a position in another state as an art teacher. I took a position as a nurse in the hospital where I had received my training, moved into an apartment, and started getting paid for going to work each day. My supervisor was supportive and complimentary. She appreciated my ability to boost patient morale and provide emotional support as well as give physical care. My own morale had been complicated by the few hours spent with Martin. After work and alone at night, during moments of introspective silence, I convinced myself that he wanted no promises and could give none. He wanted no emotional ties. He was not like Bill. Martin was so sensitive that he would not intentionally tie himself romantically to anyone until his stint in Vietnam was over.

But, I could not release the memory of our evening together. I dated others. A dinner here, movie, lunch dates. However, after climbing into bed at night, my thoughts were of Martin. And I have to honestly tell you that these thoughts were not all pure. His passionate kiss had left me breathless, wanting more. But as my thoughts ventured in this direction, the verse "Be sober, be vigilant; because your adversary the devil, as a roaring lion, walketh about, seeking whom he may devour" always interfered. I knew the devil actually existed; I had been taught so. I only hoped God would forgive me because I was so vulnerable when it came to Martin.

In the spring of 1970 as I watched the news, I learned of antiwar protests and student strikes on college campuses across the country. Many felt that Nixon was expanding the war effort. Several weeks later I heard about troop withdrawals from Vietnam with the South Vietnamese beginning to take more responsibility in carrying on the war. Where was Martin in all of this and would I ever see him again?

My feelings of depression were returning. I had stopped praying, not because I no longer believed, but because I knew not how to pray or what to pray for. I had not found a church home since graduation and only attended when visiting my parents and hometown church. Motivated to do something, anything, to get myself out of the rut I had formed, I turned off the TV, got out a phone directory and looked under "churches". From the Agape Christian Church to St. Wenceslau Catholic Church, there were three pages of churches. Special headings included Catholic, Christian Reformed, Christian Science, and Full Gospel. Having grown up Protestant, I went back to the list of Christian churches. I found St. Luke's and dialed the number to get the service times for the following Sunday.

10

I'm but a stranger here, heaven is my home. The congregation sang as I followed the usher up the middle aisle. Where *was* he taking me? I had arrived a little late and not allowed time for parking. I slipped into a pew about five rows back from the front of the church feeling like everyone's eyes were on me—the stranger here. As directed in the bulletin, I turned to page 660, the last page in the hymnal. Wondering what kind of prophecy the words should be for me, I started singing with the congregation Verse 4.

> *Therefore I murmur not,*
> *Heav'n is my home;*
> *Whate'er my earthly lot,*
> *Heav'n is my home'*
> *And I shall surely stand*
> *There at my Lord's right hand,*
> *Heav'n is my fatherland*
> *Heav'n is my home.*

The pastor walked to his pulpit to greet the congregation and give an opening prayer. A lay person read the first lesson and the second lesson. I knew the responsive verses by heart and began to feel comfortable. After the sermon hymn, the pastor returned to the pulpit and bowed his head in quiet prayer. I looked down at the bulletin and noted the sermon title, "Fellowship and the Church." God had me in mind today. The pastor cleared his throat and scanned the worshippers. I wanted to squirm. His gaze stopped ever so briefly on me, noting the stranger in his church, and began his sermon.

Fellowship? What is it? Especially… in regard to the church? Look around you. Whom do you see? I moved my head slightly to the left and slightly to the right but recognized no one. I was not thinking about fellowship, but, rather, about being the stranger. *According to Webster, fellowship means companionship, company, association. The word fellowship is listed twice. It may surprise you that the second fellowship in Webster is defined as follows: to join in fellowship especially with a church member, or the verb form, to admit to fellowship, as in a church. It may also interest you to know that the word preceding the first fellowship is "fellow servant." The word immediately after the second fellowship definition is "fellow traveler."* (He paused for emphasis.) *How appropriate when considering our walk with Christ.*

"Fellow, servant, walk with Christ." I had to admit he was getting my attention. I looked up the pastor's name in the bulletin. Pastor Williams went on to quote Hebrews 10:24. "Let us not neglect our church meetings." He used the example of how several logs burn brightly together in a fireplace. However, one log left alone on a cold hearth burns out.

Fellowship with other Christians provides relationships that are vital to our Christian growth. We need the fire of enthusiasm in our walk here on earth—our earthly home—the place that prepares us for our forever home in heaven.

Before I knew it, those around me were introducing themselves, shaking my hand and welcoming me. *Please come back, nice to have you here* comments surrounded me. I signed the Visitor's Book as I left and wrote my phone number under, "Yes, I would like a call."

One summer day folded into another and I attended church each Sunday, except on those when I had to work, and ended up transferring my membership from my hometown church to St. Luke's. There were even nights when I fell asleep, after personal devotions, with neither a thought of Bill or Martin.

As I headed home from work one day, fall leaves skirted around me and covered the sidewalk beneath my feet. For some uncanny reason, the poem I had written for Margo long ago about "leaves were falling like rain—or were they tears?" popped into my brain. I laughed, and I laughed. I was ready to let the whole thing about Martin go. I didn't know where he was. And, it wasn't that I didn't care; I was just ready to let it go. I said a small prayer that God would guide him when he returned to his life back in the states. When I got home, I took a walk. A long walk. I felt more energetic than I had in a long while. After the walk, I called Margo to see how her job as a teacher was going.

We talked for over an hour: her job, small town living, meeting someone special, her parents being okay, Martin being home and thinking about returning to school on the GI bill, and my job, transferring my church membership, and the few dates I had. We laughed about some of the silly things we had done as college students. Margo reminded me of the poem, and I told her the painting of the little girl standing in the stream was hung in my apartment living room.

"Karen, I'm going home for Thanksgiving. Will you have time off?" she asked as we wound down our conversation.

"Actually, I have Thanksgiving off and the rest of the weekend. Pretty good, huh? The bad part is that I have to work Christmas Day."

"Hey, come to my folks for Thanksgiving. Martin will be there. You met him at graduation, remember?"

"Yes, I remember." I laughed.

"Well, come, then…" she persisted.

"That's very nice of you. Let me think. I could spend Thanksgiving Day with your family and then go on to my folks for the weekend. Let me get back to you. Okay?"

"Sure, I gotta go. Papers to correct."

"It was really great talking to you, Margo."

"Call me soon about Thanksgiving," she reminded me.

"Sure, love you."

"Love you, too."

11

A long, thin, gravel road with grass growing in the middle where the car tires never tread led to an older, large, white farm house. I had been to Margo's parents' farm twice and it was as I remembered it. The corn and soybeans had been harvested. I could see as I drove the lane that the other farmers had completed their harvests, too. There were a few over grown shrubs outside the house, and the grass was neatly clipped and still green in November. A number of cars were parked around the house. Two large dogs greeted me with woofing sounds as Margo ran out to meet me. She had on an apron and greeted me with a huge smile.

"Karen, you look gorgeous." We hugged.

"You look pretty good yourself—especially with that apron," I kidded her.

"Come in. My parents are anxious to see you. And, Martin. He brought someone home with him. Do you remember Alice? She was in some of my art classes. She works....."

I didn't hear the rest of what she said. *Martin* had a girl friend. I thought I would be okay with seeing him again, but with a girlfriend? The thought of him being with someone else made me envious although I knew I had no right to be. Convincing myself that he didn't want a commitment with Vietnam and all, I hadn't thought of the possibility that he already had someone in his life. I went from feeling gorgeous to feeling stupid. I was only a few steps from my car. I could feign illness and leave now. No one would know why I really left.

"The turkey's almost done. Mom made my favorite dressing...." Margo continued her chatter.

I looked at her and smiled. I was here to celebrate Thanksgiving, to be with a friend I had not seen since graduation. I straightened my shoulders and followed her into the house.

After a hug from Margo's mom and a handshake from her dad, my coat was tossed on the bed in the downstairs bedroom, and Margo handed me an apron. I had the task of cutting Jello salad into squares.

I knew his eyes were on me before I heard his voice.

"Karen, nice to see you again. How long has it been?" Martin's hand gently touched my shoulder. I turned to see the someone I had thought about almost every day for months and months. The someone I had finally taken out of my daydreams. Behind him stood a petite girl with chin length blonde hair.

"This is Alice. She went to …."

"I know," I interrupted. "Margo told me." I put the table knife down and offered my hand. "Nice to meet you, Alice." I nodded at Alice first and briefly smiled at Martin. I could think of nothing to say, so I went back to Jello squares with shaking hands and wondered how to make the lines straighter.

Turkey, mashed potatoes, gravy, corn, relishes, cranberries, homemade rolls and the Jello squares were all carried to the large dining room table. Margo's mother invited me to sit next to Margo. Martin sat across the table from me with Alice at his side. There were a few cousins and an aunt and uncle of Margo's also present. Margo's dad sat at one end, and her mother at the other end.

"Let us pray," Margo's father announced even before we were all seated.

Margo grabbed my hand on one side and a cousin grabbed my hand on the other as the family joined hands to say the table blessing.

Come Lord Jesus
Be our guest.
Let these gifts…

Before the *Amen*, I took a deep breath and lifted my eyes to see Martin looking at me—steadily. My heart lurched and I felt a pink tinge race across my face. He remembered those feelings; it wasn't just me. He smiled quickly and winked as we all dropped our hands and started to pass whatever was in front of us.

While we ate, there was conversation of the harvest, the Farmer's Almanac winter forecast, Margo's job, my job, what's in the dressing, cousin John's missing tooth, and more. I learned that Martin was going back to college to earn a business degree from the same university that Margo and I had attended. Every time he spoke, I looked at him. His eyes seemed to linger on me. I could not look at him at other times with Alice sitting right next to him.

"We have pumpkin, pecan, or apple pie. With or without ice cream. What will you have Karen?" Margo's mother asked me.

"Pumpkin, please. No ice cream. And, I'll help." I stood up—not really wanting the pie—being too full—plus the butterflies in my stomach were not mixing well with the turkey and potatoes.

As we finished the pie, Martin pointed at me and touched his lips. I looked at him questioningly. He did it again. I soon realized that he was telling me I had pie on my face, and, embarrassed, took my napkin and wiped my lips clean.

After dinner, everyone helped stack dishes and carry them out into the kitchen. There was chatter and moans and groans about how full we all were. The sink was filled with hot soapy water and I volunteered to wash. Martin and Alice retreated to the living room to talk to the men folk. After dishes, I drew Margo aside and told her I had to leave.

"Why? You just got here," she questioned me.

I hugged her as I thought of an excuse.

"I forgot to tell you. My folks are expecting me this evening. An aunt and uncle I haven't seen for a while will be there."

"Ohhh…" She drew her eyebrows together and I noticed frown lines forming between them.

"I'm sorry. I should have told you earlier. It just skipped my mind. All the good food, conversation."

"That's okay. It's a busy time," she reassured me.

"Hey, we need to write or call more often." I said.

"No kidding. And, I do want you to meet Mark, the guy I'm seeing. Sometime. I'd like to know what you think. We're not serious. But, I think it could be. You know what I mean?"

I didn't, but I shook my head anyway. I grabbed my coat from the bedroom and hugged her goodbye.

"Please say goodbye to my family," she stopped me.

"Everyone is busy visiting. It's all right." I hugged her again and walked out to the car with Margo waving from the door. As I drove away, I looked again at the kitchen door to see Margo still waving and a taller figure behind her. Martin. And, although he was in the shadows, I detected a perplexed stare. I waved quickly and headed back down the gravel lane.

When I arrived home, Mom questioned my general pessimistic attitude. I only shrugged and tried to dismiss her inquisitiveness. "You haven't gotten over Bill," she said. I looked at her—her eyes filled with love—and thought, *it's not that simple.*

12

It was exactly one week before Christmas. The time since Thanksgiving had flown by. I walked into my apartment, and although I had just finished an eight hour shift, I flung my coat on the couch and danced a few steps. Martin was coming. My apartment was decorated: a tree, lights around the windows, and a wreath on the door. I checked my list of "to dos" before he arrived. With a hot dish in the crockpot smelling mighty yummy, I only had to toss a salad, cut some French bread, and heat up some frozen corn. I started bath water and turned on the radio.

Deck the halls with boughs of holly, Fa la la la la, la la la la
Tis' the season to be jolly, Fa la la la la, la la la la
Don we now our gay apparel

(I had laid out a favorite sweater and a pair of stretch pants in the morning.)

Fa la la la, la la la la
Troll the ancient Yule-tide carol, Fa la la la la, la la la la.

I dropped my uniform into the clothes hamper and stepped into the tub as "Deck The Halls" continued.

Fast away the old year passes, Fa la la la la, la la la la......
Heedless of the wind and weather.....

Heedless. Careless. Reckless. Oblivious. Good adjectives, I thought, for the previous three weeks of my life. At this point, a red flag should have risen, but it did not. I was in love with Martin head over heels, and I would not let logic get in the way.

Thanksgiving night he had called my parent's house asking why I had left with no goodbyes. I detected humor in his question but could not respond likewise.

"An aunt and uncle. They were here. At my folks. They wanted to see me before they left." Martin chuckled at my explanation and I felt like a small child caught in a lie.

I continued rambling. "Everyone was busy. It was easier for me just to slip out."

"And slip out you did," he finally answered. "I want to see you," he continued without missing a beat.

"*See* me? I don't understand. You did just see me." I placed my free hand over my heart to still it.

"You have a sense of humor," he added chuckling again.

I said nothing. There was silence. Maybe ten seconds. I covered the mouthpiece so he wouldn't detect my escalated breathing. Why did he do this to me? I hardly knew him, yet he affected me this way.

"Like I said," Martin interrupted the silence, "I want to see you. When are you free? Is there a night or weekend when you're free?"

I noisily pulled my work calendar from my purse. "Next weekend. Saturday. Will that work for you?"

"Sure. I know where you live. I'll pick you up around seven. We'll catch a movie or something."

"See you then," I murmured, and with shaking hands I replaced the phone in its cradle and danced around the room like a young school girl with a new crush.

The rest of the week I wore myself out with questions. Why did he want to see me? Wasn't he romantically involved with Alice? What other reasons were there? Descartes, French philosopher, considered to be the father of modern philosophy, is known for his famous statement, "I think, therefore I am." It was natural for me to gather and analyze information almost incessantly. I told myself to relax and not let my compulsive thinking ruin my chances with Martin.

When he pulled up to my apartment with a bouquet of flowers the following Saturday, I was convinced that Martin had romantic intentions. The only movie in town was *Love Story* starring Ryan O'Neil and Ali McGraw, which came to be known as the ultimate date night movie of all time. It was Martin's and my second date. We watched it once and stayed for the second showing. A story of a blissful relationship between a man and a woman with a tragic ending, I cried a bucket of tears during the first showing. I agreed to stay for the second hoping to get control of myself. It didn't happen. I had lost Bill. I couldn't help but make a connection. Martin spent most of the second showing caressing my hand and staring at the side of my face. At the time, I thought he was being sensitive to my feelings.

Martin and I didn't discuss the movie. He didn't ask *why the tears?* He drove me home in silence, put the car in park, took me in his arms and kissed me as he did that night so many, many months ago, extensively and passionately. It's what I needed. He left me limp at the doorstep as he had before—except this time, he returned.

After that evening, Martin called on most nights or simply showed up at my doorstep. He was attending university and studied at my apartment. Some nights he didn't go home. Weekends we spent together. We enjoyed the same type of music. I laughed at his jokes, typed his papers, and helped him study for tests. We just seemed to click. Martin took up so much of my life that a couple of weeks would pass before I realized I had not talked to my family or kept in contact with my friends. The relationship was consuming. I remember asking myself, *Is this what love is?* I couldn't compare it to anyone or anything else, and I stopped trying.

This particular night with the "Fa la la la ..." in the background, we planned to have our Martin-Karen Christmas. The next day, Martin would be leaving to be with his family for a few days, and having had Thanksgiving off, I would be staying to work my hospital shift.

Martin and I were watching "Hee Haw" while eating our dinner and laughing at the ridiculous jokes and skits. During a commercial, Martin turned to me and more or less blurted, "Karen, let's get married."

"Married?" I stared at him incredibly.

"Married," he answered.

"Married?" I asked again as if I had not understood him.

"M a r r i e d," he spelled for me.

I giggled. We both stood up and hugged each other. In the warmth of his embrace, I realized that although I was crazy in love with Martin, he had never told me he loved me. Nor had I told him.

I felt a passion for Martin. But, I had to admit that I hardly knew Martin. There was a part of him that I could not reach. Martin made me feel good about myself because he needed me. I had determined during the deep, quiet parts of the night when sleep would not come, that our relationship was more about Martin than me. And, at that time, I was okay with it. He needed me. I felt a sense of excitement and exhilaration around Martin I had never felt with anyone else. I refused to let logical thinking get in the way of my infatuation for this man.

"Yes?" I answered him with a question.

"Yes? What kind of answer is that?"

"Yes, Martin I will marry you." He picked me up and swung me around in circles his nose and lips nuzzled to my neck with the sounds of "O Little Town of Bethlehem" coming from the TV. Holding each other, we dropped to the couch and listened to the final verse as the choir sang.

O holy Child of Bethlehem
Descend to us, we pray;
Cast out our sin,
And enter in,
Be born in us today.
We hear the Christmas angels
The great glad tidings tell…

Martin looked into my eyes. "This is the best Christmas gift you could ever give me, Karen."

And, although *cast out our sin and enter in, be born in us today* kept replaying in my head, I answered, "This is the best Christmas gift you could ever give me, Martin."

Martin left around midnight saying he had to pack and be ready to leave early the next day. I kissed him goodbye—every fiber of my being flushed and very alive. After closing and locking the door, I noted the single package under the tree. It was for Martin! In all the excitement I had forgotten to give him my gift. I rushed to get it in an attempt to catch him before he left. While on my knees beside the tree with the gift for Martin in my hands, it occurred to me that there was no gift for me from Martin. Nothing. I put the package back in its spot under the tree, stood, walked to the window and watched as Martin pulled away into the night.

Looking out into the darkness, a childhood memory came to me. We had large evergreen trees in our yard on the farm. On a summer day, when I wanted to get away from the chores, I would hide underneath one of these majestic trees. It could've been a bright, warm, almost no-breeze day, and, yet, underneath the evergreen, I experienced a different world. It was there that I could hear the wind. It had always been there; I just had not heard it before. Sherlock Holmes in *The Hound of the Baskervilles* said, "The world is full of obvious things which nobody by any chance observes."

And so it was. I should have been excited. Martin, the man I loved, had just asked me to marry him. And yet I could not sleep. I could not sleep because tiny seeds of apprehension were taking root. When I did try to put my finger on the reasons for these tiny seeds, the thought that *love would conquer all* took over. After all, love was not supposed to be logical.

13

I didn't tell anyone that weekend that Martin had asked me to marry him because I could hardly believe it myself. We had known each other for such a short time, and it was an unexpected proposal. However, I spent every possible minute at work thinking about him, picturing myself in a beautiful wedding gown, and being his wife. During quiet times, thoughts like *Why are you doing this, Karen?* took up empty spaces in my thinking. I pushed them out of my mind along with quick but insincere prayers asking for guidance.

When he came back late Sunday after celebrating Christmas with his family, I took his hands in mine and asked, "So, what did your parents say?"

"Say?" He squeezed my hands. "About what?" He looked at me blankly and seemed distracted.

"Oh, come on…I haven't told *my* parents, yet. I wanted to tell them in person. What did *your* parents say?"

In a few seconds, I realized that Martin had not told his parents nor did he know what I meant when I had asked him, *"What did they say?"* Was it because the marriage proposal was not on his mind as much as mine? And if so, why shouldn't it be? You just don't ask someone to marry you and then forget you asked.

"I thought you would tell your parents that you asked me to marry you." I tried to keep eye contact with him, but an achy feeling was starting in my gut, and my eyes were starting to glass over. I looked down at the carpet. I hadn't noticed before what an ugly color of brown-orange it was. I wonder if we'll move I thought to myself—when we do get married.

"Karen, what's to eat?" Martin interrupted my carpet thoughts.

"I've been working. The refrigerator is empty." The achy feeling in my gut was turning to a cold, unattached feeling.

"Okay. Let's go get a bite to eat. Where's your coat?"

I pointed to the couch—the place I'd dropped it after work. He picked it up, slipped it over my shoulders, hugged me, and whispered softly into my ear.

"I wanted you to tell first. I hope that's okay."

I looked into his deep, dark eyes and convinced myself that he was being totally unselfish about this.

"Sure," I answered him timidly. "My parents, they're coming this weekend. We'll tell them together." He held my hand as we left the apartment. It was wintry cold. Ice crystals stung my face as I walked to the car, and the wind tore at my unbuttoned coat. I felt childish. What was wrong? Nothing, I convinced myself. I was tired, and I had spent Christmas for the first time in my life alone and without my family. Don't blame Martin for your bad moods.

After pizza, Martin brought me back to the apartment. He went on to his own apartment saying he had unpacking and studying to do. He hadn't hit the books at all over vacation. I locked the door behind me, took off my coat and hung it carefully in the entryway closet. The place was dark and quiet. I flipped the switch that turned the Christmas tree lights on and noticed that Martin's gift from me, a brown, v-neck, XLT, sweater, was still under the tree. I picked it up, walked back to my bedroom, opened the closet door and stashed it back behind my shoes where it had been stored for many months.

Laden with grocery sacks and my Christmas gifts, my parents arrived on Saturday morning around 10 a.m. I was cooking spaghetti and had French bread in the oven.

"Karen, what's wrong with you?" My mother always read my feelings. I had never liked it. I could never be alone with my feelings around her, she read me like a book.

"Me?" I opened up the refrigerator and grabbed lettuce, tomatoes, and some onion for a salad. "What do you mean?"

"Are you feeling all right?" She took the vegetables from me and carried them to the sink.

"Sure, Mom. It's the first Christmas I haven't been home. It just all seems a little odd."

"Of course. We really missed you," she sighed. "But, we're here today."

"Martin will be over in a few minutes." We both worked at the salad.

"Okay. What is it with you and Martin?" She took a hold of my shoulders and turned me to face her.

The warm fuzzy feeling for Martin returned, the feeling that came when I wasn't being analytical.

"Well, let's just say we have some news for you." My heart quickened. I couldn't help it. We were getting *married*.

"News? That sounds serious, honey. Do I have to wait?" She was chiding me, and yet I could see concern in her eyes.

12:00 noon came. 12:15 came. Martin did not.

"Let's eat," Dad said from the living room. "I've been smelling that spaghetti and garlic bread since mid-morning."

I went to the window. No Martin. He said he would be here. Not wanting my parents to see my frustration, I pulled the French bread from the oven and announced, "Time to eat!"

I left Martin's place set at the table, but as the minutes passed, it was only a sad reminder that he had not showed up on one of the most important days of my life—the day I had planned to tell my parents of our marriage. My parents and I exchanged gifts, visited about Christmas at home and my work. Dad took a nap while Mom and I attended to the dishes. After a couple of hours, Dad looked at his watch and eyed my mom.

"Best be getting' home, Mom." He turned to me, "Did you say that Martin fellow was going to be here today?"

"Yes, Dad. I'm not sure what happened. I hope he's okay."

"Sure do, myself." He yawned and started walking to the coat closet. "The weather's supposed to turn bad tonight, Mom, so we best be on our way."

Mother eyed me cautiously. She was trying to read my feelings, and I was trying not to let her know of my worry and frustration. I busied myself in the refrigerator with the leftovers attempting to send some home with them. She had always done a good job with that.

"Don't bother," Mom stated. "Dad and I need to cut back, especially after the holidays. Don't we?" Dad pulled Mom's coat out of the closet.

"What's that?" He asked, trying to remove the hanger from the coat.

"Oh, never you mind." She slipped her coat on, kissed me goodbye, and turned to take my father's arm but not before I noticed the tears in her eyes. Mothers always know too much.

Slipping on my warmest coat, stocking cap, and gloves, I left the house in late afternoon to walk. After several blocks, I started checking surroundings. Houses were still lit with seasonal flair. In front of an aging home, a miniature Mary and Joseph were standing against a sagging porch. Mary held her son wrapped in swaddling clothes against a cold winter afternoon. Joseph's hand was on her shoulder as they stood on frozen ground surrounded by last fall's withered weeds. How depressing. Their eyes were downcast. Taking a closer look, I noticed that Joseph's hands were weather-stained, and part of baby Jesus' ceramic blankets were chipped and resting at their feet. We all lived in such a broken world. I could not leave this forlorn picture feeling as I did. I searched my desperate soul asking God for something to hold on to.

The verse my college professor shared with me after Bill's death came to mind. "We know that in everything God works for good with those who love him who are called according to his purpose."

I thought of Jesus' life and how difficult it was. He was born in a barn to parents-on-the-run, grew up a carpenter's child, encountered lepers, ate with prostitutes and tax-collectors, and although he performed miracles and met human needs, he constantly contended with skeptics. All of this took place in a dusty, backwards world. Eventually, he carried a wooden cross after being whipped and left bloody; he was nailed to that very cross and executed. He did it all for each of us. Out of love.

The only thing that could pull me back from the emotional turmoil was love. Love of God. Love for my fellow man. Love for myself—for I *was* created in his image.

I left Mary, Joseph, and baby Jesus as they were, but came away somewhat enlightened. The load was lighter. I didn't know where Martin was or why he didn't show for my parent's visit. It was something he simply refused to discuss when he did return. I understood that there were parts of Martin I would never understand, but I also knew that with God's love, I could survive whatever life threw at me.

14

Martin and I got married in June. Back then, almost everyone got married in June. And, that was the only thing normal about my wedding. It was not the wedding of my dreams; it was not the wedding my mother had imagined, I'm sure, for her only daughter.

Being brought up as a regular church-going family, my parents took it for granted their children would be married in the church. Martin refused saying all the fuss and all the people would make him uncomfortable. He wanted a simple wedding. With an aching heart, I left the apartment after that particular conversation and headed toward The Falls Park, the hideaway I had often ventured to during my college days. It was dusk. Feeling burdened, I slowly got out of the car. Slowly and carefully I walked over the rocks and got as close as I could to the spraying water without getting soaked. I felt a cool mist cover my face. Soon, hot tears blended in. I dropped to my knees in prayer.

"Dear God, What am I to do?" Coughing up sobs, I didn't even know what to ask, and so I asked for forgiveness. I had not included God in this plan. Why had I never prayed about a life companion, a mate, a husband? And here I was planning a wedding. An hour later, I picked myself up and headed back to the apartment. I did not have a solution but did realize that it was up to me to stay connected to God, my Father. I felt stronger on the way home and started singing parts of hymns from the past. "Onward Christian soldiers, marching as to war…." I smiled. Where did that song come from? Please, God, I chided, what are you telling me?

Martin met me at the door. I had expected him to be gone.

"Karen? What's wrong? Where have you been? I've been worried." These were unusual questions for Martin, so unusual that I had no response.

"What's wrong?" he repeated.

"Everything, and maybe nothing," I answered, not making any sense.

He tilted my chin up. "Everything? Nothing? You're going to have to explain that one."

"It's the wedding. My mom always thought I would get married in a church. And, now....well, you know.... You don't want to get married in a church, and..."

"Karen, where did you go?"

"What do you mean?"

"Where did you just go?'

"To The Falls Park. It's where I go when..."

"Let's get married there. We'll have a minister. Invite a few friends. What do you think?"

I took a deep breath and remembered the spray on my face. "It might just work, Martin." His unpredictability delighted me and, at other times, sent me into a tail-spin.

"Martin, will you pray with me?" I asked him cautiously.

"Pray? Why?" he questioned me starting to withdraw.

"I'm not sure. It's just that marriage is a big step in our lives. It wouldn't hurt to ask for God's guidance."

"My faith is personal. Let's keep it that way." His head dropped as he folded his arms across his chest. I didn't want to ruin the moment and I could live with his suggestion to get married by the falls, so I dropped it.

And so on June 20, 1970, with the sound of the water hitting the rocks behind us, I became Mrs. Martin Christiansen. Martin's family and mine were present. Margo stood up with me, and my oldest brother stood up with Martin. A few friends also attended. Later, we all enjoyed a buffet meal at a local restaurant where my parents had reserved a private room. We opened the few gifts: a fondue pot, a knife set, a pottery service for six, and glassware.

It was during the dinner that I overheard a conversation that astonished me. It was a conversation between our parents.

Martin's dad was saying, "It was over 20 years ago when we took the little guy in. What was he, Miriam? Three, four years old? Couldn't have been much older. We wondered if we were doing the right thing. Well, it hasn't always been easy...but I think we did the right thing."

"Martin was a beautiful child," Martin's mother continued the conversation. "We fell in love with him immediately. He's had that little patch of white behind his ear ever since we've had him."

My mother caught my eye. I could see a big, invisible question mark on her face. I smiled at her and slightly nodded as if I knew all along that Martin had been adopted, when, in reality, I knew nothing about it.

Notes taken from an anatomy class suddenly flashed before me. Our bodies hold trillions of cells containing genetic material. This blueprint of traits and characteristics are so complex that if you were to write out its components, it would stretch from the North Pole to the equator. Part of this blueprint comes from Mom; part from Dad. It's the combination that makes us unique. No wonder I had never seen a family resemblance between Margo and Martin. I looked at Margo carefully wiping her mouth with a napkin. Why hadn't she told me? And, did it, would it, make a difference?

"Karen will be so good for Martin. He needs a stabilizer in his life. Someone to love him," Miriam continued.

I studied Martin's parents. Genuine. Loving. Hoping the best for their son.

I looked at Martin who was visiting with my brother. I studied the side of his face where his sideburns ended. I noted the gray streak behind his ear and the slight crinkle around his eyes and thought, *this man, Martin Christiansen, is a stranger to me.* I twisted the gold ring on my finger and started to slide it off. I was *Mrs.* Martin Christiansen. Why hadn't he told me that he was adopted as a child? What else had he not told me? Uneasiness snaked through me like a lightning bolt. I looked down at my plate of food so no one would see the tears forming and excused myself. I walked until I found an exit door and stepped out into the sun. I felt so weak, so pessimistic.

"For heaven's sake, Karen," I declared out loud. "This is your wedding day!" I quickly looked around to make sure no one had heard me. There were probably lots of things Martin had not revealed to me. Just as there were lots of things I had not told Martin. Like Bill. I had tried to bring Bill up but, most of the time, Martin was not interested in my past or what I wanted to talk about. We had a lifetime to discover each other. I smirked at my silliness, turned, and walked back to our reception. Martin was waving me into the room—people wanted pictures. It was good to feel his warmth as we stood with our arms around each other saying cheese as the flashcubes blinded us, one picture after another.

The honeymoon? Martin had told me he would take care of it. After the reception, we hopped into my decorated Pontiac and headed down the street with Martin at the wheel.

"So, wife, where are we headed?" Martin pulled the veil off my head and ran his fingers through my hair. I felt a hint of despair, took a deep breath, and reminded myself to stay positive.

"You're going to surprise me, aren't you, sweetie?" I reminded him.

"Well, let's just head out of town and see where we end up. You've got cash, right?" He winked at me and squeezed my hand as he brought it to his lips. After a few caresses, he continued to grip my hand as he brought it down and placed our folded hands on his right thigh.

"Sure," I quietly replied. I turned to look out the back of the car. No friends, no family was in sight. I was alone with Martin. I wished otherwise. I imagined myself at home with my parents, sitting on their worn couch and eating popcorn while watching Lawrence Welk. After all, it was Saturday night. I felt and wanted Martin's passion, but for some reason, on this my wedding night, I wished I were elsewhere.

Martin turned the radio on and sang along with Tom Jones, "Sugar Pie, Honey Bunch…can't help myself, I love you and nobody else," and I started to relax. About 20 miles out of town, we stopped at a motel with a pink vacancy sign flashing. Martin dropped my hand and ran his hand alongside my cheek and down the side of my dress. He asked for cash before jumping out of the car. Pulling a few twenties from my purse, I felt absurd. The pink flashing vacancy light discolored my white wedding dress. Everything felt tight—my dress, my shoes, my undergarments, my heart. A mosquito was buzzing somewhere in the car. I looked down at my lap to see clenched fists and immediately released them. Martin's voice interrupted my thoughts.

"Karen, come on. Get your stuff." He stood in the front of the car with a wide grin. I opened the car door and retrieved a small suitcase from the backseat. Martin had packed nothing.

We walked into a room with possibilities. A soft lamp lit a corner of the room; the bed looked clean and had a floral spread; the clock ticked 10:50 p.m. on the nightstand; an air conditioner provided a quick relief from the humidity. I placed my overnight bag next to the bed, slipped off my shoes, and sat on the edge of the bed. Martin's eyes had grown intense, dark—one of the things that had drawn me to him when we first met.

Although we had been staying together off and on, we had never slept together. I thought it unusual that Martin had never pressed the issue. Choosing to think of it as an attribute of his—his respect for me—we never discussed it although it seemed a contradiction to his zealous nature about so many things. I had never asked him about previous relationships.

He was so mysterious about some things. He had never offered to tell; I had never asked.

He softly closed the door. I walked towards him and put my arms around him. He returned the embrace and whispered, "I've never felt loved by anyone as much as I have felt loved by you. You're my wife. Can't believe I'm married."

"It's true. It really happened. We're husband and wife." Looking into his dark eyes, I kissed him tenderly.

"Take your clothes off," he almost demanded, smiling.

"What?" I replied. I hadn't read many romance novels, but I didn't think it was supposed to go this way.

"Karen, take that thing off."

"Umm, I thought, maybe you'd....."

"My fingers can't begin to work those buttons. Just take it off." He kissed me, again, long and steady, and I felt the heat of his body mix with mine.

I couldn't tell if he was being playful or starting to get agitated. So, feeling like a disobedient child, I took off my wedding dress and placed it carefully at the foot of the bed. He stared at me briefly, picked me up, and gently laid me on the bed. I had day-dreamed about this moment with Martin for months. I was apprehensive and yet eager. Martin and I consummated our marriage at 11:15 p.m. Minutes later, with tears covering the pillowcase and my right arm across his chest, I listened to the clock tick-tock and watched Martin as he slept soundly.

Passion is one thing. Love is another. They are not one and the same although one can love passionately. Martin was filled with passion. I wanted to be loved....and so, we spent our wedding night.

We returned to the apartment and the orange-brown carpet the next day. I unpacked the suitcase and found places for our few gifts. Martin headed off to the college library to get some work done. He was behind, he complained. I popped some popcorn and snuggled under a blanket on the couch with the TV news moderator for a companion. A Vietnam War orphan was being adopted into an American family and becoming a citizen of the United States; something about President M. Nixon, Henry Aaron, Ella Fitzgerald and Louis Armstrong. I stared at the screen blankly. Even though it was June, I was cold and sleepy.

My Bible caught my eye on the lamp stand by the couch. I reached for it; it had been so long since I had spent time reading it. I opened it randomly and read from John 16:33, "...in the world ye shall have tribulation..." and didn't like it. I flipped to Proverbs 23:7, "For as he thinketh in his heart, so is he…" and liked this better. I knew a pessimist sees life as being difficult and an optimist sees opportunities even in difficulties. This was my first whole day of being Mrs. Martin Christiansen and here I was home alone dressed in an old pair of stretch pants and large sweatshirt snuggled alone under a brown and tan afghan made by my grandmother. Something was wrong with the picture. But I remembered the tightness of everything the night before and for some reason, home alone felt better, and soon drifted off to sleep, open Bible in my hands.

"Julie, Julie, wake up," Martin gently shook me. "What are you doing out here? You need to come to bed."

"Martin, you're home," I spoke without opening my eyes. I had been in a deep sleep. "Where were you?"

"I've been in bed," he chuckled, "waiting for you. Come on, sleepy head. I left you alone when I came home, but it's the middle of the night. You'll sleep better if you come to bed."

"Sure." I opened my eyes, and Martin and I walked arm in arm to our bedroom. I dropped my stretch pants and sweat shirt to the floor and crawled into bed while Martin went to the bathroom. Seeking warmth, I stretched my limbs to his side of the bed but found none. My eyes popped open in realization. Martin had not been in bed. His side of the bed had not been slept in any more than mine.

I listened to the water turn off and on several times. Brushing his teeth. Toilet flushing. He left the bathroom and walked out to the kitchen. I heard water running, a pill bottle being opened, the sound of pills tumbling out of a plastic container, water running, and then his footsteps padding back to our bedroom.

He climbed into bed, sighed and drew me into his arms.

"Martin?"

"Yes," he breathed in deeply.

"What time did you get home?"

"I don't know. I guess I didn't look at the clock. I was tired, climbed into bed and thought you'd come. When I woke up, you weren't here, but you are now." I could hear the smile in his voice. He wrapped his arms around me and kissed me. His freshly brushed teeth could not mask the smell of alcohol.

"Where were you?" I murmured.

He released his firm hold and sighed. I detected a sense of exasperation.

"Studying. I told you before I left. You go to work each day, come home, and can forget about it until you go back the next day. Which reminds me—you didn't even go to work today. Have you forgotten what it's like to be a student? I got behind with all this wedding stuff."

He released me, rolled over and brought the covers up to his chin.

"Please don't be angry. I just missed you."

"Julie.... Don't think that just because we are married...." He started and then stopped before continuing. "You're not always going to know where I am. I'm not going to always know where you are. We are two adults. We have separate lives." He paused. Even though his head was on the pillow, I could see it turn from side to side in an *I can't believe you* implication.

I rubbed his top arm lightly. "We're both tired. We'll talk tomorrow."

I left my hand on his arm and soon sensed him to be asleep. His breathing was even. His body was relaxed. I turned over and faced the wall and brought the covers up to my chin with clenched fists. A few tears escaped. I wiped them away with the back of my hands and folded them in prayer.

"Dear Heavenly Father. I come to you without knowing why. I know I am to give praise and thanksgiving. But, there is none within me. Forgive me for this. I am unworthy, yet I know you love and care for me. Thank you for this. I don't understand Martin. I don't understand my own feelings. Was this marriage not a part of your plan? Is it me?"

15

"Honeymoon" is a trip or vacation taken by a newly married couple or a period of harmony immediately following marriage. If you call an overnight stay in a dingy motel twenty miles away from your wedding site a honeymoon, then I had it. However, there was no way that a period of harmony existed in our home.

My soul needed harmony. I had read somewhere that one cannot strive to please another by distorting one's soul. I soon realized that I would need courage and an extra measure of compassion to be in a relationship with Martin. I didn't know if I was strong enough.

The yearning for love was a vital and healthy need. I had seen the positive and negative results of good and bad relationships with the patients I cared for. Those who felt loved, those patients who were visited and nurtured and cared for, those patients who were eager to go home to loved ones healed more swiftly in comparison to those who were not visited, who were not cared about. These patients were often pessimistic about their condition and life in general, and they were typically not easy to care for. Nurses were in and out of their rooms quickly, whereas, it was easy to linger in the rooms of those patients who had family at home who were eager for their return. Sick or healthy, we all desire, even ache, for the same thing: someone who cherishes us; someone who loves unconditionally, someone who will laugh and cry with us; someone to come home to; someone to sit on the couch with —even if there is nothing to be said; someone who knows and understands you better than anyone else in the world. Good relationships not only call for harmony, but cooperation and sharing. A part of sharing is the ability to care.

I felt cheated. I knew it was a sin to think such thoughts, but I could not make them go away. During my positive states, usually at work and busy with patient care, I would not think about Martin at all. When I did, my mood lowered. At times, I thought it was the devil at work. Had

I not taken marriage vows "for better or worse till death do us part?" My family did not believe in divorce. Why was I thinking of it? I had not even given my marriage to Martin a fair chance. After all, only recently he had returned from a war zone—Vietnam. I could not imagine all that he had been through. I remembered May, 1970, the day students in an anti-war demonstration at Kent State University were gunned down by the National Guard. What must Martin think when he hears of these demonstrations? He never cared to talk about any of it.

Without giving you a listing of wrongs, I can simply tell you I became the poison arrow target. Some of my co-workers complained of lids left up on toilets, caps off toothpaste, and dirty socks left on the bedroom floor. I sometimes stared in disbelief. *These* were problems? I had recently married and was living with a man who randomly threw injurious remarks about my behavior or looks. A man who complained about the temperature of a meal or the fact that he worked much more than I did. And ask *was this all we had to spend this month?* A person who spent my income but had none of his. A man who asked me to leave the apartment so he could study. Or, simply ignored me, telling me nothing, showing his back when I wanted to talk. At these times, my brain lulled to mush and then transformed itself into thinking sinister thoughts and deeds. I frequently prayed for forgiveness. The reality of being human and weak was in my face constantly. Needless to say, my self-worth plummeted. I tried to tell myself it was just Martin; he was having a bad day. No matter how I tried to de-personalize it, I never succeeded. His looks and words stuck to me like flypaper.

Besides the injurious remarks, lying and insults, there was a greater problem. Martin was a petty thief. I found miscellaneous things like socks, a men's manicure set, flashlights, pens, a Twins hat in my car or under the bed—new items with no sales slips or sign of a shopping bag. Whenever I questioned him about these items, he would ignore my question or say someone had given them to him. I was afraid he would be picked up as a shoplifter. Thoughts of the embarrassment it would cause both of us haunted me, but I felt helpless to change any of it.

Gone was the wonder of new love I had known in the first few months with Martin. There had been excitement, fascination, passion, a sensitivity of sorts. I was becoming obsessed with fault-finding. The physical intimacy with Martin I had dreamed of before marriage was non-existent; we only had physical contact in the dark of night. It always came unexpectedly and with no conversation. After the act, we were soon asleep our backs turned to each other.

As my perceptions of Martin changed, my perceptions of self changed. I often felt angry, left-out, pessimistic, and generally old. I missed the wonder of life and love we had first experienced. Again, I felt cheated. Martin's behavior might have been suspect, but I was certainly not fun to be around.

I could make a list of Martin's peculiarities. And, believe me, I did so mentally dozens of times. I told myself that if I understood his behavior, I could deal with it. But, I never did. Because of who Martin was and what he did and because of who I was and how I responded, each time we fought or disagreed or misunderstood, I changed a little. I withdrew. I placed the feelings deep down, self-contained. And, when another episode occurred, I brought them all out, gathered them round and let the anger brew until the ugly claws of resentment made it difficult for me to love him or for him to love me. I felt deserted. Consequently, I was coming from a place where I could not help him.

While listening to "Creation Moments" on Christian Broadcasting radio station one day, I learned of the mimic octopus—an animal so new to science it has not even been classified. This animal, capable of many disguises, may take on the appearance of a flounder and even swim like one. The minic octopus has been observed acting as a starfish, jellyfish, giant crab, seahorse, and other creatures. It has the ability to morph from one animal to another. This skill puzzles scientists as such high intelligence evolves only in social animals, and octopuses are solitary creatures. The creator, as "Creation Moments" explained, gave it the intelligence it needed to survive its predators.

Since trying to understand Martin had become a major time-consumer, of course, I thought of him. Did Martin consider me a predator of sorts? Did I cause him to be apprehensive? He seemed to be doing a good job of morphing and doing what he pleased—both inside and outside the relationship. Like the boogey man underneath my childhood bed, was I looking for something that wasn't there? Was my perception twisted? Or was he simply Martin, a man with some difficult issues he was trying to work out on his own. Each of us has our own spiritual journey. None is alike.

My headaches were worsening. The front window of my car was hit by a small, sharp rock once. It made a slight indentation at the time, but by the next day, fine lines had ventured forth. In a week, these fine lines took on a spider-web existence filling most of the windshield. My headaches were like that. Starting small, growing until my head felt like a cracked egg with my usual, rational, courteous self oozing out like the white of the egg. The usual over the counter pain killers didn't seem to help.

One Saturday while picking up house-hold clutter and gathering clothes to wash, I found a note in one of Martin's pockets. *Martin, you know how I feel about you. Why do you keep pulling away from me? … SE*

Martin was not at home. I knew that if I asked him about the note he would say it wasn't his, he found it, and wonder why I had reason to not trust him. I was tired of being angry all the time, but this was a last straw. After much brooding and debating, I made an appointment with a therapist. I had to talk to someone. Entering the office, I noted new office furniture and an attempt at cheeriness. On the wall beside the receptionist desk were nicely framed and matted quotes.

The whole is more than the sum of its parts. Gestaldt

Another read:

If I'm frantic, life will be frantic. If I'm peaceful, life will be peaceful.

…and, yet, another….

Fear is the absence of love.

Already worn-out by my own, excessive thinking patterns, I slumped in a chair, chose a blank wall to concentrate on and thought about counting sheep. I didn't want to sleep; I just wanted to clear my head.

Dr. Feldt smiled kindly, took a few notes as everything tumbled out. After my lengthy monologue, he put down his pencil and said, "Karen, I'm glad you're here. We can help you, but most of all, you need to know that you have everything you need to help yourself."

He explained that depression is a feeling of intense sadness which may follow a recent loss or other sad event but is out of proportion to that event and persists beyond an appropriate length of time. Grief, loss, separation from the death of a loved one, divorce, or romantic disappointment can cause depression.

"You've had a double-dose of these kinds of events in your life and occurring in a relatively short time period. You need time to heal." Dr. Feldt explained kindly.

He recommended a marriage counselor and didn't think medication was necessary but did agree to follow up with an appointment after I had counseling. I made the appointment for the following month and felt somewhat relieved. I was taking steps to remedy whatever.

On the way home, I considered how difficult self-perspective is. One minute, I think I'm created in God's image and loved with an incredible love, precious in his sight. The next, I realize what a mess my life is and feel like a filthy rag having failed myself and God. There's good and bad tangled up in all of us.

Martin was home on time for supper. We had hamburgers and hash browns, not my favorite, but I knew Martin would enjoy them. He helped me stack the dishes in the sink and then snuggled on the couch to catch the news: the Twenty-sixth Amendment was extending the right to vote to 18, 19, and 20 year olds; President Nixon; space exploration; and "Ol' Blue Eyes" Frank Sinatra's retirement. I listened barely. It felt good sitting next to Martin shoulder to shoulder, hip to hip, feeling his warmth. We could talk. I would tell him.

"Martin?"

"Yea," he answered—his focus on the television.

"I'm going to see a counselor—a marriage counselor."

"What?" He mumbled. "Listen to this, the Bears lost again. Can't believe it!" He got up from the couch, flipped off the television and headed for the kitchen. I followed.

"I went to see a therapist today. He suggested I see someone. I haven't been much fun lately, and to be honest with you—I know it's affecting our relationship. It's something I think I need to do. For us." I was making an attempt to shoulder the responsibility for the feeling of separation between us and not wanting to alienate Martin even more but hoping he would take the hint that we really needed to do this.

"Sure. Do what you need to do. I won't stand in the way. A *psychiatrist?*" He asked pointedly as if he had furtive information. Martin chuckled and pulled me close taking a nip at my ear.

"You are one crazy lady," he articulated clearly between kisses. I didn't know whether to feel insulted or relieved. Instead of seeing a need to work on the relationship, he seemed to be empowered with this new tid-bit of information. When he kissed me tenderly, however, I melted. I so strongly wanted to believe in love. I hugged him tightly, but he pulled my arms away.

"Gotta go, honeybun," he stated matter-of-factly. "Got a study group. Meeting at the library. Test tomorrow." Without a second look, he grabbed a few books and a light coat and headed out the door. I heard the engine start on my Tempest as I walked to the living room window. Standing in the evening shadows, the car lights swept over me as he backed the car out and headed down the street. Gone. Just like that. Silence. Not wanting to give into anger, wanting to stay positive, wanting to remember the warmth of his kiss, I walked into the kitchen and busied myself with supper clean up. I tended to the laundry and ironing and made sure my nurse's shoes were clean and white for the next day. I looked at the clock. Nine o'clock. I picked up a few newspapers, read a chapter of a book I wasn't really into and prepared a warm bath. Ten o'clock.

16

After bathing, I put on a new nightgown and climbed into bed hoping Martin would be home early. I had to be at work the next day by seven. I turned my face to the window to count the stars when I saw it. A falling star! I hadn't seen one in years. It was both awesome and ominous. Feeling restless, I threw off the covers, pulled on an old pair of pants and tee shirt. Grabbing a lightweight jacket from our front closet, I headed out into the night.

I headed toward the campus having no idea what I might find. I just knew the library was closed at this hour. Taking the most direct route and walking briskly, I spotted my car parked on a side street about six blocks from campus. Music came from a coffee house nearby. I walked in. The front entryway was a short, unlit hallway. I stood in the semi darkness and scanned the room. Someone with a guitar was strumming on a small make-shift stage. About a dozen persons were at various tables in deep conversations. As I turned to leave, I heard his voice. Martin's. I scanned the room, again. In the corner of the room I spotted Martin sitting with a blonde. She looked familiar. Alice? Alice, from Thanksgiving? I felt myself being shoved forward as a large group entered the coffeehouse, chattering and laughing. I turned to leave, not wanting to be pushed into the light of the room and exposed.

My anger was incomprehensible. It was not raging anger; it was nauseous anger. It was an uneasiness that made me feel like running, yet my feet felt as if huge weights were attached. My senses were in slow motion. As I rounded the corner of the coffee house to begin my journey home, I noticed a small, narrow window. Looking in, I saw, not five feet from me, Martin and Alice. Martin had her hand in both of his and was looking into her eyes and talking. Talking. Something he rarely did with me.

Jael Heber's wife, in Judges, took a hammer in hand and went softly to Sisera, another man, and smote a nail into his temples, and fastened it into the ground. Although her circumstances were different than mine, I thought of this story and knew how she could do it. I wanted to kill Martin in some horrendous way.

Martin never came home that night. I did not sleep. I did go to work the next day. It was the only place I could go. I did not want to be home when Martin did come. I would've wanted to ask questions. There would be no answers, only lies, or silence, or a turning around and leaving.

On day overlapped another. Monotony at its best. Martin carried on as usual—going to classes and coming home when he pleased—sometimes for supper together and at times not coming home at all. He never explained his whereabouts, and although you may think it strange, I never asked. People always say—talk it out, don't let the sun go down on your anger. Sensing that *talking it out* would irreparably damage our relationship, I grew quiet. Along with growing quiet, my anger and bitterness also grew—a huge, cold stone of resentment affected my every waking moment.

Those at work noticed my behavior change.

"Something's wrong; talk to me," my co-worker Brenda insisted. Weakly smiling, I continued with my patient care.

"You need to get out more," another chided.

"You might be right," I answered. If they only knew.

While I was reading up about cardiac care at home one evening, the phone rang. Martin wasn't home. I tossed the blanket covering my lap on the floor and rushed to the kitchen to answer it. We didn't get many calls.

"Hello."

"Hi, Karen? It's me, Margo. I haven't heard from you in ages."

"Margo? Wow, it's been a long time." I hadn't seen her since our wedding.

"I sent you a birthday card and wrote you another time. Are you okay? It's not like you…."

"You did? I'm not sure I…."

"You sound funny. Karen, what's going on?"

Looking out the small window of our kitchen, I thought about hanging up. I hadn't talked to anyone about our marriage. How could I start now with Martin's sister, my friend.

"Are you still there? Karen, talk to me!"

Turning from the kitchen window with downcast eyes and phone in my hand, I glimpsed the worn, orange-brown carpet and started to weep. If I hung up, Margo would only call back, or worse, make the long drive to our house. I had to talk to her. But, how could I? Martin was her brother.

"Everything is so wrong," I started.

"Have you been hurt? Did you lose your job? Where's Martin?"

"Martin's not here. I'm not sure where he is…"

"It's Martin, isn't it?"

"Margo," trying to speak between sobs, "I don't know what to do. I'm living with a stranger. I'm so sorry, he's your brother, but things are going very badly. It's not what I thought it would be—this marriage…"

There was silence at the other end. Thinking I had offended her, I mumbled, "I'm sorry.…"

"No, Karen, I'm sorry. I should have told you. We should have talked before you decided to marry Martin. But, you seemed so happy, and Martin did, too. I thought this, this marriage, might fix everything."

"Fix what?"

"I'm not sure where to start. Let me see; I'll drive up tomorrow. Can we meet at your apartment? It'll be around 3. If Martin is there, we'll go for a drive. Is that all right?"

"Sure. Thanks, Margo. I'll see you tomorrow."

Replacing the phone, I heard the front door open and close. Quickly wiping my wet face with the back of my hand, I headed toward the bathroom to wash my face. Closing the door behind me and turning on the light, I looked at my reflection. Evidence of pain, resentment, and stress had left traces.

"Karen, I'm home. What's to eat around here?" Martin rummaged through the refrigerator.

"I'll be out in a minute." I powdered my red nose and swollen eyes in an attempt to hide misery.

"There's meat cuts and cheese if you want a sandwich."

"…had one of those for lunch. Why would I want another?" he answered.

"There's left over spaghetti. It's at the bottom of the fridge."

"What do you do all day? When is the last time you cooked?" He actually looked at me as I came out of the bathroom and I felt ashamed about my appearance.

"What do you do all day?" He demanded as if I were a child.

Dumbfounded, I stated clearly, "Martin, you're never home. How would I know when to cook?"

He shook his head, grabbed his coat and started toward the door.

"Martin, stop!" I heard screaming and realized it was me. He looked at me—somewhat puzzled. "What's the matter with you? What happened to us? This is not a marriage. I don't even know you." Our ship was sinking and I felt helpless to stop the waves from crashing over the sides.

" I don't know what you're talking about. Look at you. You're a mess. I have classes, tests. I want to finish college. Get my degree. What kind of support have you been? Nothing! You're not the person I thought I married, either." And he was gone.

It was the most Martin had said to me in weeks, and it was hideous. Lies. I didn't know what to think; I didn't know how to feel. I never saw my parents argue. I knew they disagreed at times; they just endured these disagreements and life went on. It was that simple. This thing between Martin and me was complex. I couldn't even begin to sort it out. If someone had asked, "What happened? When did it all go wrong?" I would have no clue. It was just that—all wrong. I could not talk to him. I did not understand him. And, the worst of it was that he didn't seem to care or take an interest in me, his wife.

With a monstrous headache, I headed for the bathroom, took two aspirin, ran a hot bath and turned on the radio. I needed to clear my head, get some sleep.

Sleeping fitfully, one dream followed another, but I remember one in detail. On a pontoon boat with people I didn't know, I was riding up front when a strong wind and dark clouds foretold of a coming storm. The waves grew and splashed water into the boat as we sped across the lake. The other passengers shrieked with excitement as the boat started to sink. I stood and jumped into the lake thinking the boat was no longer a safe place. Huge waves doused me and I began to sink due to my heavy clothing and shoes. Treading and treading, my arms became weary as the boat disappeared while the occupants looked at me astonished.

The following Sunday in church the sermon title was "Keep Your Eyes on Jesus." Our pastor quoted William Cowper from *Light Shining Out of Darkness*. "God moves in a mysterious way his wonders to perform. He plants his footsteps in the sea and rides upon the storm." I couldn't help but think about my own dream in which I jumped overboard during the storm and slowly felt myself sinking with the waves smacking my face while I gulped for air. My human instinct—was it to jump ship during the storms of life?

The children's sermon was about Peter walking on the water. Peter did fine, you may remember, until he took his eyes off Jesus. When he started checking out his surroundings—boisterous wind, crashing waves, gloomy sky—he started to sink. He had lost faith by losing focus on Jesus.

Pastor summarized that day by telling us that God sometimes calls us to do impossible things by faith so He can receive glory. We need to keep our eyes on Jesus in every aspect of life.*

(*Adapted from *Keep Your Eyes on Jesus* as told by Rev. Lewis Shaffer, Son Shine Ministries International Inc.)

17

Margo arrived in the afternoon. We hugged and looked each other over closely.

"You're gorgeous," I honestly told her. Margo was still single. She continued to teach art classes in a small town and do volunteer work at a museum. She was seeing someone but not seriously. I envied her. Her life seemed so simple.

"You look tired and worn-out," she answered.

I grimaced. "I'm sorry." She hugged me, again.

"Tell me what's going on. It's Martin, isn't it?"

"It's Martin. It's me. It's our marriage. It's all wrong and I don't know why."

Closing the front door behind us, we walked together to the couch.

"Can I get you something to drink? Lemonade? Coffee?"

"Coffee. Black. Sounds good."

Margo quietly walked around the living room while I started the pot. When I returned to the living room, she made eye contact for some time as if considering carefully her words.

"Martin's different, Karen. Our family always knew it. I wanted to believe that marriage would help him. I couldn't warn you ahead of time. You were in love, and I really thought it might work."

"What would you have said to me?" I questioned. "Before we got married, that is."

"Well," she paused. "Like I said, our family always knew Martin was different. My parents adopted Martin when he was a little guy. I was younger, but we all enjoyed his good looks, his energy, and he was so bright. He picked up on everything so easily. We thought he could do well in school, but he had problems. Staying in for recess, failing tests, not getting along with others. That kind of thing. My mom used to hate to go to the mail box—too many letters from that school, she would say. No matter how hard my parents tried, Martin was never close to them. Mom and Dad were glad when he decided to join the service—thought it might help him grow up, as Dad used to say."

Smiling, I admitted that even if Margo had told me all that I would have married Martin. He was so handsome, so warm, so funny; there were times when he was hard to resist.

"There was that part of him, too," Margo smiled. "It's just that those closest to him never seemed to see that part of him. It's what happened in our family. Now, it's happened to you. I'm really sorry, Karen." She grabbed my hand and squeezed it. She went on cautiously, "I overheard my parents talking once—I had gone to bed—gotten up—it was very late. It was a quiet conversation. Something about Martin being abused by his mother as a child. It didn't mean a lot to me, then. I sensed we had rescued Martin, that his home situation was not good. As an adult, I'm beginning to understand the impact it perhaps has had on his entire life." Margo turned and looked out the window. I didn't know what to say.

She suddenly stood up, "Want to get a bite to eat? I'm starving."

After a shake and fries at the DQ, Margo prepared to leave. "You can tell Martin I was here, if you like. Just tell him, I stopped in. Tell him hi."

"Where do I go from here?" Knowing she wouldn't have an answer, the question still needed to be asked.

"I wish I knew. You need to see someone. Like a marriage counselor. Although, knowing Martin, he won't go. But, you need to go. You need to take care of yourself. This is not good for you." Weakly, she smiled—an attempt of encouragement.

She drove off and I felt more isolated than ever. "This is not good for you," she had said. Checking the key holder, but not really needing to, I knew that Martin had my car. He sold his car saying we needed the money although I never saw it or heard how he had spent it. Grabbing a sweater and turning off the lights, I locked the apartment as I left and headed towards The Falls Park.

The Falls Park was the place where Martin and I had exchanged our vows just months earlier—*for better, for worse, till death do us part.* This was the place I ventured to while in college when I needed to get-away and collect serenity. Since I loved the outdoor, earthy smells, the spray on my face, and the sound of rushing water, the experience somehow changed my perspective and helped me see things more clearly. Stuff that seemed impossible to get through became surmountable.

It was early evening. Garage doors opened and closed as parents arrived home from work. A mother or two stood on porches beckoning children to supper. A dog barked in the distance. There were a few shops on this edge of town: a small grocery, a snack shop and a pawn shop. Stopping to eye the curiosities, I noted a wall hanging entitled, "Old Chinese Proverb." Stained and discolored from age, it read, "A woman should be like water; she should take no form and have no voice." I looked around; the streets were completely empty. I read it again. "A woman should be like water; she should take no form and have no voice." I laughed. Not a good laugh. Martin would ditto this one.

Thoughts about our relationship, thoughts about Martin, *questions* about Martin filled my head and gave me no peace, only agitation. A psychology class covering Pavlovian theories about intermittent stimuli popped into my head. Rats had to press their noses against a button to get food. The first set of rats got food whenever their noses pushed a button. The second set got an electric shock along with their food each time their noses pushed the button. The third group of rats, sometimes got a shock with their food, but sometimes did not. Which group fared the worst? The third set. Why? The rats with intermittent shock were the rats who chewed their tails up, gnawed away at their fur, and then sheared their skin by rubbing against their wire cages. They even ate their own feces. The bottom line regarding the study was that inconsistency was the single most destructive force on the rats' psyche. I wasn't a rat, but I understood the connection to my own life. Martin's inconsistent behavior was taking its toll. The ignoring, the rebuffs, the sarcasm, the never knowing when he would be home or not intermittently mixed with the precious moments of genuine silliness, shared laughter, and emotional intimacy caused me to remove myself little by little until my love for Martin was failing both of us. Emotional atrophy. Romantic tragedy.

Remembering that I had not really prayed about the relationship to begin with, I took a deep breath and prayed asking God to let me see Martin through His eyes.

I passed an old movie theater with *Baby the Rain Must Fall* printed boldly on the marquee. I remembered Steve McQueen's character—mixed up-- for no apparent reason-- married to a sensible woman who seemed *not* to want to know any answers. Maybe I cared too much. Maybe I was too reactive. Maybe my expectations were out of line. Maybe.

Continuing my walk, I crossed some railroad tracks to the "watch-out" part of town as we named it in college. It was the poorer part of town, the wrong-side-of-the-tracks side. Residents from here were apt to show up in the emergency room late at night with cuts, bruises, and occasional broken bones or knife wounds due to family or neighborhood squabbles. The houses were small and worn-out looking. Often the roofs were sagging and the paint peeling. Toys cluttered the dirt yards. Broken down cars propped on cinder blocks sat in the front yard or blocked the alleys. Loud conversation seeped through the walls. Was it TV or family squabbles? As I turned right to the park entrance, I realized a car had been following me. The driver stopped and allowed me to walk across the street. Lifting my hand in a slight wave, I made eye contact and felt a cold feeling grow deep inside. Stuffed in a plaid flannel shirt, the driver was huge, had a cap pulled down over his forehead, and gave me the creeps. Feeling weak in the legs, I continued through the park entrance and felt some relief after I heard him speed off shifting gears carelessly.

Sitting on a rock next to the falls, I noted the low water level. The grass around the falls was brown and brittle. Wrappers from fast food joints, a beer bottle, and picnic left-overs littered stagnant water. The place was desolate and gloomy. What an ironic analogy—my life and the river. I thought of the saying, *misery needs company*. Although I was tired of crying, the tears started, flowing down hot cheeks. Margo's words, "This is not good for you," came to mind. I thought it would be good—coming here. Placing my head on my propped up knees and closing my eyes, I kept sobbing.

Much later, I realized how late it was. It was a moonless night, totally dark except for a street light at the entrance. However, as I raised my eyes to the heavens, the stars were beautiful, breath-taking. I took a deep breath and felt a hint of hope. Remembering my long distance runs at night when I lived on the farm made me think of my parents, growing-up, and the unconditional love they gave us.

Needing to get home, I headed toward the park entrance. It was not only dark but deathly quiet. Each step and each breath I took could be heard. About twenty yards from the park entrance, I spotted it—the same car I thought might have been following me earlier. It was a junker, of sorts, with rusted sides, dark and dented, parked under the entrance light. I had to walk by it to get out of the park. Feeling apprehensive, I looked inside as I passed. There was no one. I quickened my step, and at that very moment, someone grabbed me. From behind, he wrapped his thick arm around my neck and chest, picked me up off the ground and threw me into the front seat of his car. His bulk followed as he pushed me to the floor of the passenger side.

"Don' move lady and don' say a thing. We're goin' for a ride." Margo's words came to mind once again, *this is not good for you.*

He had to have been sitting in the darkness waiting for me—watching my every move. The crying, the sobbing—an easy victim.

"Don' even think 'bout gittin' out, sister. I got a gun, and I'll use it." His voice was thick and husky, strangely quiet.

A spot under my eye felt hot and sticky. I was in a twisted position; my spine rebelled and my chest area was on the way to a heart attack. Face to face with a grimy floor mat, I could see nothing. However, I could smell: alcohol, urine, and sweat. B.O. is what we called it in high school. *He has B.O. Don't go out with him. He's nice, you know, but he has B.O. This is not good for you.* Margo, driving home. Martin, where are you? .. till death do us part…My parents at home watching TV. Random things. The children's sermon about Peter walking on the water: don't lose focus, Karen. Focus on Jesus. I visualized Peter expressing the shortest prayer in the Bible, "Lord save me," Jesus stretching out his arms to help, and a certain calm washed over me.

Other questions whizzed through my brain. *Can I get up? Where are you taking me? What are you doing? Who are you? What's wrong with you?* However, not wanting to know the answers to any of them, I prayed continually.

Although The Falls Park was near the edge of town, there were several stop lights before getting completely out of town. When the car stopped, I would have to open the door, get out, and run. I turned my head slightly to detect over-head lights. He was speeding through them. With his meaty hand on the gearshift, he had to be going 50 miles per hour in town. I could only hope for a policeman to be nearby. In a few minutes, I knew there would be no more stop lights and no more town cops. I tried to relax my body by taking deep breaths. His breathing grew heavier, almost asthmatic.

"Sista, hope ya in for a good time. Looks like ya need some company— cryin' like that. What's tha matta with you, anyway?" He chuckled and pawed at my back. I started to squirm to a sitting position, but with his meaty fist he squished my face into the grime of the floor mat.

"Ya ain't goin' no where—less I says ya can. Got it, sista? We're goin' for a ride, a nice ride. I think ya like it. Might even make ya feel better. You ain't in good shape now, anyway." The car turned onto a gravel road. Dust crept into the car crevices and into my nose and eyes. Not more than a half mile down the road, he slowed, pulled over and stopped.

"Beer in the trunk. Remember, I got a gun, ya try anything…well, ya know what I mean. Sit tight."

Acting on survivor instinct, as soon as his door slammed shut, I bolted up and out of the car. The ditch was steep and I fell into it, but I was soon up and running up the backside and over a barbed wire fence with the barbs tearing at my palms and legs as I scrambled over. I heard him fume as the trunk slammed shut. He had his beer, but he didn't have me. If he had a gun, he wasn't using it; at least, not yet. As heavy as he was, I could outrun him. I struck out—through the cornfield. I knew about cornfields. I had grown up with them.

The corn was over my head, and as I ran, the dry leaves whipped at my face and arms. Every twenty feet or so, I switched corn rows and ran until I could run no more. On hands and knees, I tried to still my heavy breathing, listening, listening. A light breeze rustled the leaves. A field mouse scurried past me. As I stood up slowly, I felt it: the slight rumble of a car traveling inaudibly at a snail's pace down a gravel road. But where? He had turned off the headlights. I headed further away from the road, walking slowly this time and listening, but I heard only the wind's nightly sighs.

Soon a farm yard light appeared about 200 yards away, and I headed in its direction. Looking from side to side before entering a new row, my alarm system kicked in when I realized this creep had turned on his headlights and was using them to search the rows of corn. With lights streaming across the tops of the corn tassels, I crouched and waited. Within minutes, the lights swished away, and the car sped down the road at an alarming speed. I stood erect, but exhausted, and watched the tail lights diminish in the distance. Knocking on a farm door, calling a friend from work for a ride, filing a police report, going home to an empty apartment finished my night.

The next few weeks were rough. I had experienced a new kind of fear, and I found myself afraid of persons and places that had never bothered me before. Going to church was the only mainstay in my life. A verse from Isaiah 64:8 caught my attention one Sunday. *Yet, O Lord, thou art our Father; we are the clay, and thou art our potter; we are the work of thy hand.* On another Sunday, I heard a reading from Paul's letter to Titus…*At one time we too were foolish, disobedient, deceived and enslaved by all kinds of passions and pleasures. We lived in malice and envy, being hated and hating one another. But when the kindness and love of God our savior appeared, he saved us, not because of righteous things we had done, but because of his mercy.*

The next few months passed in a haze. I told Martin about the abduction—as the police called it. Martin moved out: it was his way of coping or it gave him a good reason to leave. I gave notice at the hospital, packed all my belongings, cleaned the apartment, and made the trip back to the farm. Needing time to sort things out, to understand so many things that had happened, and preparing for a court appearance, I thought it was the best place for me to be. My parents welcomed me with open arms. Feeling like the prodigal son, I moved into my old room with the flowered wall paper, chenille bedspread, and throw rugs. The painting, a gift from Margo at graduation of the little girl in aqua shorts by the beginning of the Mississippi River, hung on the wall beside my bed.

After the usual farm breakfast of an egg, toast and jam, and Mom's homemade cookies, I helped Dad with the few chores he had and then helped Mom with mending or with any number of her many little projects. We visited; we watched the news; my brothers stopped off and on. I started running the lane again, and after a few weeks, ran the section. I always ran during the day. Gazing into a night sky filled with stars gave me an uneasy feeling. It would take time for me to no longer feel like a victim of a crummy circumstance. A letter came from Margo. Martin had re-enlisted. Her parents learned that he had received no credits while attending college. Apparently he had been attending classes but had not taken tests or finished the required work. She wrote that she was sorry a half dozen times. She was responsible in no way for my situation.

18

"Calvin Wilson, remember him?" My mother pointed to his name under "elders" in the bulletin. "He's an elder. I don't know how he got it. But, he is…" my mother whispered to me and the two rows behind us. We were in church; it was Palm Sunday. With my mother to my left and my dad on my right, I was between the two people who loved me most in all the world. Yet, I felt very alone.

The congregation rose to sing the opening hymn, "Jesus, Refuge of the Weary." Although the hymn was not familiar, the tune was and I began to sing, "Jesus, refuge of the weary, blest redeemer, whom we love. Fountain in life's desert dreary, Savior from the world above. Oh, how oft Thine eyes, offended, gaze upon the sinner's fall. Yet, upon the cross extended, thou dids't bear the pain of all." With an ache in my heart, I could sing no longer. The congregation started the second verse; I heard the phrases, "thorn encircled brow, sinless death, life eternal, peace, rest, grace, calming the sinner's stormy breast."

The pastor interrupted my thoughts.

"Jesus didn't come to make it better for us here on earth….our perceptions are not his….His journey to the cross was with the intent to save us from our sin. His intent was to offer salvation. Because of his love for us, he saves us from the curse of eternal death." I knew that Jesus' death on the cross was a gift given in love. And, yet, at this point in my life, I felt too unworthy to be a recipient.

As we waited to receive communion that day, I noted the cross draped in purple and black. I believed. I knew the truth, yet my heart was hard. Before the prayer of the church, the congregation sang: "Lord be my consolation, my constant source of cheer; remind me of your passion, my shield when death is near. I look in faith, believing that you have died for me; your cross and crown receiving, I live eternally…"…and I asked myself, "Where is your joy?" I was disconnected from Jesus Christ, my Savior and

King, but it didn't need to be a long road back. That very night, I got on my knees beside my childhood bed and asked God for forgiveness telling him that I accepted him as my Savior. I also gave thanks for the many blessings I had: loving parents, good friends, the farm, and all of my many experiences. I had to believe that as time passed these various experiences would make me strong, would develop my character. So, I gave praise.

"Sunrise, Sunset…." There's a song…I'm not sure who sang it or why, but to me it was about time passing. One day after another: tedium at its best. Emotionally, I thought I was healing. Mom and Dad's unconditional support got me back on my feet. My parents, however, could not help me with another problem.

A group of small painful blisters followed the itching, tingling, and soreness I was experiencing in the genital area. When it became difficult to urinate and walking became uncomfortable, I made a doctor's appointment. As a nurse, I had helped examine women with sexually transmitted diseases never thinking I would have to deal with one myself.

"Looks like genital herpes to me. We'll send a swab to the lab to make sure, but I'd bet my bottom dollar…., " he rambled as he wrote. Then, he turned and looked at me directly, "You're a nurse, Mrs. Christiansen--it is *Mrs.* Christiansen, right?" Nodding slowly, he went on, "..then you know that we can not cure this. We can reduce the number of outbreaks with antiviral drugs which you must get started on right away. If not treated, serious complications are possible. . .but rare." He looked out the window although the blinds were folded and pushed his heavy, black square glasses back up his nose and frowned. "Also, you'll need to inform your sexual partner of this genital herpes in hopes that we can prevent the spread to others. Any questions, Mrs. Christiansen?" Without waiting for questions, he continued talking as he wrote, "I'll write out a prescription for you. You know that you can infect others even when you are having no symptoms as you are today. You might want to check back with me in a couple of weeks."

He cleared his throat, finally looked at me, and left the room. The nurse entered, told me I could get dressed, and that I was *free* to leave. Free? I could not move, let alone get dressed. My body simply would not respond. I sat on the examining table and stared at the white examining room wall. There was a height chart, a weight chart, and information on cardiac disease prevention. The words were all a blur. The same nurse entered the room and asked me if I was okay. I could not answer her. I could not even look at her. Okay? I would never be okay again.

Isolating myself in my bedroom that evening, I skipped supper, lay on top of the chenille bedspread, and played with the possibilities of a letter to Martin.

Dear Martin,
  Hi. Remember me? You have a venereal disease. You need to see a doctor soon.
  Sincerely,
  your first wife....

  Or....

Hey Martin,
  You won't believe this one. Of course not. You have a venereal disease. I suggest you let everyone know.
  Just me, ...

  Or....

Dear Martin,
  I heard you re-enlisted. Forget about the idea of "a girl in every port." Cause, it's not going to work for you. Say, hello, to venereal disease!
  Thought you'd like to know,
  Me

After idiotically playing with ideas, I realized I needed to tell Martin in person or by phone call. Being a nurse, I understood the responsibility of dealing with a sexually transmitted disease and protecting others. Martin, however much I hated him at this moment, needed to be told.

Mom quietly knocked on my door and let herself in. Sitting at my bedside, she felt my forehead as if I were her young child.

"You have a fever, don't you? Did you say you saw the doctor today?"

"Yes, Mom, I did. It'll be all right." I tried not to look at her.

How could I tell my mother that I had a sexually transmitted disease? How could I tell her I might have to be on a low dose of antiviral drugs the rest of my life? Even with the drugs, recurrence was possible. What would she think? She kept looking at me as if trying to read my mind. She always knew when I had my period as a teenager. It always annoyed me; could I keep nothing to myself? But this? Mom was innocent, perhaps naïve. Did she even know what a sexually transmitted disease was?

Taking her hand in mind, I repeated, "It'll be all right. Just a bug." A bug that could *bug* me the rest of my life.

The following night, after calling Margo and getting a phone number of a base camp in Mississippi, I dialed the number. Interestingly enough, I was quite calm. With everything that had happened, not much else could go wrong. It was a relief to me at this point that Martin was far away. Deciding to take the high road, I planned to visit with him about reenlisting, and then carefully inform him of the venereal disease, the steps he needed to take for personal treatment and for protection regarding future sexual partners.

Even though we were together as a married couple only for a few months, I should have remembered the unpredictability of his personality and been more ready for his reaction.

He answered the phone after the fourth ring, already annoyed.

"Hi, Martin, it's me, Karen."

"Who?"

I attempted to soften my voice and hoped it would help him feel less threatened as I repeated, "It's me, Martin. Karen."

"Sure, what is it? I've only got a few minutes. Where'd you get my phone number?"

"Margo gave it to me. I hope that was . . ." I hesitated sensing his agitated state. "We need to talk."

"Make it quick—like I said I've only got a few minutes."

"…so, you reenlisted. I hope that works out for you."

"No reason it won't. You called because…?"

"I called because I went to the doctor today and was told that I have a venereal disease."

"You what?" He sounded puzzled—like he was trying to figure something out but soon went on, "What does that have to do with me?…. Listen, I've got to…"

Interrupting and raising my voice, "Martin, stop and listen. This is important."

"You having a … whatever-you-called it disease is not my problem. That's what happens when you walk the streets after dark. You should have known better. Any self-respecting…"

"Martin, I got it from you." There was momentary silence.

"That's the biggest lie I've heard in a long time. You're a tramp. I can't believe you'd stick something like that on me and make me responsible for…." I stopped listening. I could no longer endure the insults and lies. I did not understand where Martin was coming from; however, I felt that he was twisted in some strange and significant way.

"Martin!" fury and exasperation had to be evident. "You need to take care of yourself and think about protecting others. Get some help!" I hung up.

Although it was an ugly exchange, I felt empowered. I would not play the role of a victim. I had informed Martin and knew what I needed to do to take care of myself to remain as healthy as possible.

"Karen, are you all right?" My mother walked into the kitchen. "I heard you shouting. What is it, Karen?" She gently hugged me. "Let me help you," she whispered tenderly.

"I'm okay Mom, really. I just needed to talk to Martin. I'm going to be all right." I tried to convince myself as much as her. "There's going to be some changes, but I will be okay."

"You know, honey, you can stay as long as you need to. Dad and I will help you through this."

"I know you will. You've always been great parents. It may take a while, but things will get better."

Managing a weak smile, I hugged her and took the steps two at a time up to my room. Getting out a pen and paper, I made a list. I would contact a lawyer tomorrow about a divorce or possible annulment. I would change my attitude around home and be more of a positive support to my parents with their daily chores, and, meanwhile, look for a job and, possibly, an apartment or house to rent. I needed to get back on my feet and out on my own.

Martin had his own life journey to live out in some way with or without me. I would try to be loving in the worst of circumstances. And, so I prayed, "Dear God, help me forgive him even though I do not want to."

I picked up my Bible from my dresser and turned to a bookmarked page. 2 Peter 1: 5-9 and read.

For this very reason, make every effort to add to your faith goodness; and to goodness, knowledge; and to knowledge, self-control; and to self-control, perseverance; and to perseverance, godliness; and to godliness, brotherly kindness; and to brotherly kindness, love. For if you possess these qualities in increasing measure, they will keep you from being ineffective and unproductive in your knowledge of our Lord Jesus Christ. But if anyone does not have them, he is nearsighted and blind, and has forgotten that he has been cleansed from his past sins.

And I prayed again thanking and praising God, for I knew that He was always with me and had provided these particular verses for me at this particular time.

19

The sign above the table read, "REGISTRATION." Dressed in practical shoes and a professional skirt and jacket, I sat at a table and handed out health forms for the upcoming school year. It was late August, and I had been hired by the Adams' Community School District as the school nurse. Since the school district was a small district, I would be serving kindergarten through twelfth graders. Slivers, small scrapes and bumps, sprained ankles, hangnails, cramps, missing mom, tummy aches on test days and more would all be a part of my agenda. The nurse's office was a 20 by 12 foot room with two army-like cots on one end with curtains that could be drawn for privacy. There was a small refrigerator between the cots. On the other end, a sink, a cupboard for medications, a desk, and a file cabinet furnished the room. A small bathroom with its own door was at the far end. Prior to registration, I had enthusiastically decorated this room with health posters and an ivy plant on the file cabinet.

Finding an apartment in the same town and moving out from under my parents' care had become an August project. My life was slowly, but surely, returning to some kind of normalcy. Getting to know the school secretary, Cheryl, the principal, Mr. Grafft, and the school counselor, Bruce, became my first priority. We would be working in the office complex together and in one of my classes I had learned, that "good relationships make things work." Being an expert on a bad relationship, I wanted to get off to a good start. Being new in town, these relationships were the only ones I had, until the school year started and the children started pouring in.

"Mrs. Christiansen? Is that your name? It's what's on your desk? I can read."

"You're almost right. If you say 'Ms.' Instead of 'Mrs.,' it will be perfect." I knelt down to get on the level of this curly blonde with sky blue eyes and a dimple on each side of her smile.

"What can I do for you today?" It was the first day of school. Cheryl had told me that the first week would be slow. They're all so eager to get back she had told me. They won't get sick for a while.

"Well," the little blonde drawled out her 'l's, "Let me see, I think I have a…... loose tooth. That's it, a loose tooth."

"What's your name? I'll need to get your file out." Looking her over, I wondered why she needed my attention. Dressed in off-brand blue jeans and a white tee shirt, I noted that she was clean and healthy looking.

"Liddie, that's my name. What did you say yours was?"

"Christiansen. Ms. Christiansen. Can you remember that?"

"Sure, but I can read; I'll just look at this," and she pointed at my name plate positioned in the corner of my desk.

"It's great you can read, Liddie. Christiansen is a long name and you read it perfectly. Now, what's your last name?"

Liddie put her finger on her chin and rolled her eyes upward as if to think. Before coming up with an answer, she dropped her finger, turned, waved, and blurted, "I've got to go now; I'll be late for math."

Coming out of the nurse's office, I asked Cheryl, "What was that all about?"

"Oh that's Liddie Meyers-Jenkins. She's in here often. Needs a lot of attention. Not sure why; she's cute and bright besides. Lives with her dad part time and her mom part time."

"Interesting little girl."

"That's what almost everyone says—interesting. Myself, I think she's a bit of a mystery. Something is missing with that child. She'll be in to see you often."

"Thanks for the heads-up, Cheryl."

And so the first day began. A paper cut, a couple of headaches, and several teachers in for aspirin filled my day along with sorting files. After school, I made a point to get out and mingle with the staff. Wanting them to be on a comfort level basis with me and knowing how completely filled their days were, I took the initiative to make contact.

"Diane, how was your first day? Bet the kids were all glad to be back." Diane, the fourth grade teacher, and close to retirement, smiled with her lips, but exhaustion covered her face like a cream.

"If only I had their energy," she sighed. "Most of them go home pumped up to come back tomorrow. Me?" She laughed. "I've got to get a better vitamin, I guess."

"Laura, how's it going?" I questioned the 5th grade teacher as I continued my hallway walk.

"Going, going, gone…the day's over and we are off to a running start. These fifth graders act like ninth graders. They get bigger ideas every year."

"What a challenge," I tried to sympathize. "How do you do it?"

"Good question. One day at a time. That's all I can do."

I finished the first week having learned all the teacher's names and positions, and had somewhat of a start with the few students who were becoming regulars at my office door for various reasons. In between the visits, I continued to review files. Even though it was a small town in a mid-west environment, I was amazed at the complexity and dysfunction in many of their lives, complexity and dysfunction that resulted from choices adults in their lives had made—unaware of the possible impact they would leave for generations.

Trying not to take my concerns home with me, I joined a yoga class and took weekly trips to the small library to read both fiction and non-fiction. Dorothy Garlock's historical fiction entertained me while giving me an idea of what life was like in early America. *Walden and Other Writings*, by Thoreau, provided an insightful view of a man who was stoic, frugal, celibate, and yet delighted in life. He constantly found reasons to celebrate: finding wild meadow flowers, drinking from a cold forest pool, studying an afternoon sky. Thoreau was both inspirational and immensely complex. Another book, *Growing Up Female in America*, edited by Eve Merriam, encouraged me to be more brave and less intimidated by my circumstances. Merriam shared stories of Elizabeth Cady Stanton, Arvazine Angeline Cooper, and a mountain wolf-woman of the Winnebago Indians.

In the late fall of my first year as a nurse with the Adams County School System, I also joined a church. It was one of two in town, and Cheryl had invited me.

"Please come, we need new members. We have a new pastor. You'll like him."

And, I did.

From the first reading from Isaiah 55: 1-9.…

"Ho, everyone who thirsts, come to the waters;.…let them return to the Lord, that he may have mercy on them, and to our God, for he will abundantly pardon. For my thoughts are not your thoughts, nor are your ways my ways, says the Lord. For as the heavens are higher than the earth, so are my ways higher than your ways and my thoughts than your thoughts."

...to the second reading from 1 Corinthians 10: 1-13...

I do not want you to be unaware, brothers and sisters, that our ancestors were all under the cloud, and all passed through the sea, and all were baptized into Moses in the cloud and in the sea, and all ate the same spiritual food, ..."

....to the baptism of baby Jacob whose four rows of relatives beamed and smiled as the church gave the baptism response, "We welcome you into the Lord's family. We receive you as a fellow member of the body of Christ. A child of the same heavenly father and a worker with us in the kingdom of God."...

...I was hooked. Feeling at home in the midst of fellow believers, I started to recall Sunday School stories and confirmation verses. Pastor Paul was spiritual, genuine, and caring.

It was in church, several Sundays later, that I noticed Eli—the quiet, little fourth grader who came to my office daily for his medication. It was late November, close to Thanksgiving. As the wind whipped the remaining leaves outside, we worshipped the Lord inside. Recognizing his slight stature and dark, thick hair from several rows back, I studied the man next to him. Very tall, with Eli's dark, thick hair, he was dressed in a black sweater and gray dress slacks. During the sermon, he placed his arm around Eli and occasionally rubbed Eli's back with his well-manicured fingertips.

Following, *Praise to God, Immortal Praises,* the final hymn, I waited to leave. Eli and his father turned in their pew to retrieve their coats. I caught Eli's eye and waved slightly. He shyly smiled and returned the wave.

The following day, Eli Wilson walked into my office with a smile on his face.

"Eli, guess who I saw yesterday?" I questioned.

He wrinkled his brow and then questioned, "Me?"

"Sure was."

"I didn't know you went to our church, Ms. Christiansen. I would have waved before if I had known."

"No problem, Eli. I just started going to your church several weeks ago. Pastor Paul is great isn't he?"

"Yea. He's new, but our other pastor was good, too. He used to come to our house after my mom died." Eli's shoulders shuddered as he tried to stay upbeat. "Yea, he was nice. He tried to help."

"I'm sorry about your mom. How long ago was that, Eli?"

"I better get to lunch Ms. Christiansen."

87

As I handed him his medication and a small plastic cup half full of water, he looked up at me and said, "I was seven years old." He placed the pill on his tongue, gulped the water, turned and left the room.

Later that afternoon, I questioned Cheryl about Eli's family. Learning that his mother had died of breast cancer several months after her own mother, Eli's grandma, had died of the same disease, I was filled with sympathy for this small boy who had lost so much.

"He's an only child. His father is devoted to Eli although he doesn't always attend conferences. I think he still feels vulnerable—Eli's father, that is. There's that haunted look he carries around; he didn't used to have it. Eli's mother was beautiful, not from around here, though. When they moved into the community she became involved in lots of things here at school, at their church, and in the community. Tons of people at the funeral."

The phone rang and Cheryl turned to answer it. Returning to my office, I pulled Eli's file. I had perused all files before the start of the school year, but needing to view more carefully its contents, I picked through Eli's file.

Since Eli was on medication for ADD, the school nurse needed to complete a yearly healthy plan. I reread it to make sure everything was up to date. Attached to the plan was an article, "Dr. Shorten Answers Your Questions. ADD: Look for These Symptoms." Dr. Shorten used information from Hallowell and Ratey's book "Driven to Distraction" to list 20 symptoms evident in persons with ADD or ADHD. I skimmed the list: a sense of underachievement, difficulty getting organized, trouble getting started, trouble with follow-through, easily bored, easily distracted, low tolerance for frustration, impulsive, tendency to worry needlessly, insecurity and more. However, on the positive side, the list had "often creative, intuitive, highly intelligent." My heart went out to this little boy who seemingly had more to deal with than most his age. As I continued through his file, I noted the Individual Education Plan that was implemented with some modifications and accommodations to help ensure that Eli would be successful with his classroom work.

I walked to the outer office and looked through the row of windows to the cafeteria where a line of middle schoolers waited in line for lunch. Where was Eli? I could smell the tacos—a school favorite. Some students were seated and chatting non-stop while eating. Others were still in line. Giggling, some minor pushing, the usual middle school stuff. As I wondered if Eli had disappeared into the bathroom before lunch, I found him. Seated at a round table, by himself, with no lunch, he stared out a nearby window. I left the office, approached his table, and sat down.

"Eli, where's your lunch?"

He turned and smiled slightly.

"You don't like tacos; is that it?"

"Tacos are okay. I don't like standing in line, so sometimes I don't eat." He sighed deeply.

"Who do you usually sit with when you do eat?" I asked wanting to know more.

He stared at me briefly and went back to looking out the window.

"Look, Ms. Christiansen. There's a squirrel, a gray one out there. We don't see many like that."

"Hmmm, I see him." I tapped his arm slightly so he would look at me.

"Tomorrow, I want you to plan on eating and the next day and the next day. You're a growing boy, Eli; you need those calories."

He raised his eyebrows. I couldn't tell if he felt threatened or surprised that someone cared enough to talk to him about his needs.

"I mean it Eli. I'll be watching you to make sure you do." I pointed to the office windows to let him know I had a front row seat on what happened during lunch time.

"OK. Tomorrow, they're having pizza. I guess I could eat that."

"That's the plan, Eli."

Standing up, I wanted to ruffled his hair or bend and give him a quick hug, but we were in the middle school cafeteria, and I knew he didn't need that kind of attention in front of his peers.

"I'll see you tomorrow, Eli. Have a good rest of the day."

As I returned to the office, Cheryl smiled at me knowingly.

"I see Eli is not eating again," she mentioned while filing papers.

"Hopefully, he will tomorrow. Let me know if he's not. I plan to keep an eye on him."

20

Away from work, I went through periods of time when I could not stop thinking about Martin. Like Dorothy from the "Wizard of Oz," I had followed the yellow brick road only to discover that the wizard was not at all what he first seemed to be. Disappointed and in anguish, I wanted to feel sorry for myself. Bitterness, like a leech, was constantly trying to drain the good in me. I had a pleasant, nurturing childhood which had left me somewhat naïve. But, my relationship with Martin and the emotional basket dumped in my lap disturbed me more than anything else in my life.

And, the memories of Bill always came as if I couldn't have one without the other. If I had just said yes to Bill when he asked me to marry him, Martin would have never been in my life. If Bill had told me about his faith in God, it might have made a difference.

One morning, after a night of tossing, turning and wondering how I could have been so unknowing, and asking all of the "why me" questions, I threw back the covers and walked to the front door and out into the cool morning air. Lifting my arms, I pictured myself flying. I wanted to feel light, carefree and young again. I wanted to giggle. I wanted to dress up and have a man look at me with love and desire. The romantic idea of love, intimacy, forever companionship had escaped me. In my heart of hearts, I knew I could forget Martin only by forgiving him and becoming spiritual in every sense of the word. Lifting my eyes to the sky, a single tear warmed my face as it drifted down my chin. With a prayer on my lips, "I forgive you, Martin, although I do not understand," I ventured back into the house, picked up pen and pencil and wrote.

I can forgive; I can forgive.
With God's help, I can forgive.
I chipped away at the resentment
In the cold dark corner of my heart.
I can forgive; I can forgive.

With God's help, I can forgive.
Until the cold, dark corner softened,
And there was nothing.
Nothing.

....

Not able to think of how to finish this poem, I grabbed another sheet of paper and started a letter.

Dear Martin,

It had been many months since I had talked to him—the telephone conversation regarding the sexually transmitted bug. What could I say? *Hi, it's me Karen. How's life? Have you messed up anyone else's life?* There was the resentment showing up in my thoughts, again. I smiled slightly as I remembered recently treating my apartment with bug spray for little spiders and other unnamed creepy, crawling things. The next morning, they lay lifeless on the floor. I took several tissues and wiped the residue off the floor, tossed them into the toilet and flushed. Several days later, there they were, the descendants of the lifeless creepy crawlers, hatched from some unknown place and thriving. Resentment was kind of like that. I thought I had taken care of it, and there it was, showing up again, thriving and just as creepy as ever.

Dear Martin, I tried again.

I am currently working as a school nurse and liking my job. It offers different challenges than my job at the hospital, but I am enjoying it. I hope you are okay with your decision to go back into the service. I'll have to get your address from Margo as I am not sure where you are stationed. You are probably wondering why I'm writing. I need to let you know that I forgive you. It was a mistake—us getting married. I need to ask for your forgiveness, too. It doesn't seem like we were meant to be together; however, I was not always loving and understanding. Hopefully, we can both put this relationship in some kind of healthy perspective and go on.
I will keep you in my prayers,
Karen

I reread it, took a deep breath, folded it and inserted it into an envelope. Sealing it with a lick, I considered that Martin would actually be touching this envelope. This thought both repulsed and softened me. Would he read it and think about what could have been or would he simply toss it aside with yesterday's trash? Would he even open it?

91

Interestingly enough, the following Sunday's sermon was about forgiveness. As the soloist sang in her deep alto voice, "When it looks like you've lost it all and still don't have a prayer, Jesus will still be there," I surveyed the congregation looking for Eli's dark head. I discovered it just two rows ahead of me to the right. He was snuggled next to his dad—Eli's head resting on his dad's arm.

Pastor Paul interrupted my thoughts with verses from the Bible. "... My grace is all you need for my power is greatest when you are weak. I am most happy, then, to be proud of my weaknesses, in order to feel the protection of Christ's power over me. I am content with weaknesses, insults, hardships, persecutions, and difficulties, for Christ's sake. For when I am weak, then I am strong." Thanks to Pastor Paul, I started to see my dilemma with a new perspective. My circumstances were an opportunity for me to grow in Christ. I left church that Sunday feeling less like a victim; it was a burden lifted. I also left with a feeling of expectancy. It was a good feeling, a giggly kind of feeling that something was right around the corner somewhere—and designed just for me.

I finished the school year with a lighter heart. Keeping an eye on Eli and watching him grow emotionally stronger gave me another focus. Liddie visited me two to three times a week. She needed to connect with me; I wasn't sure why, but I detected a sadness in her beyond her years. There were, of course, the daily medications to dish out; the bandaids; the conferences behind closed doors regarding pregnancy scares and family abuse; but all in all, the days passed quickly. I slept peacefully each night and greeted each new day with a certain amount of joy.

In the spring, Margo got married. I was her maid of honor. The wedding took place in a country church surrounded by fields about to be planted. On that day, birds were in song and the smell of earth was fresh and new. I watched Margo and her new husband, Frank,—the way they studied each other during their vows, the warm touches, the special smiles and whispered comments exchanged and felt happiness for Margo. However, I hated to admit this—even to myself—there were pangs of jealousy and heartbreak for what I did not have. Love was real and thriving. I could not predict their future, nor could I have predicted my own. However, today was filled with adoration and no one, no matter what the future brought, could change that.

Although the minister of this small country church was a man of small stature with a voice to match his size, every ear was alert to his message. He spoke of the "great wonder" of marriage. In Ecclesiastes 4 he read, "Two are better than one because they have a good reward for their toil. For if they fall, one will lift up the other... Again, if two lie together, they keep warm; but how can one keep warm alone?"

Quietly he spoke of being bonded in one flesh so that love, dreams, goals, and even spirit ultimate in an intimate companionship, and this is all possible because "God is love." Because God is love, and in marriage, two are committed to love each other, we should nourish and cherish each other daily. There was a sense of exuberance and renewal —not only for this newly joined couple--but for the many couples of various ages who left the church hand in hand.

Martin was an usher in the wedding. The night before, at the rehearsal supper, we shared a quick *hi*. It had been a couple of years since I had seen him. He looked older, was heavier, and came alone. His facial features carried a bit of sadness, and I noted he was often alone with a drink in hand. I thought about approaching him and asking how he was; however, he had not responded to my letter, and I didn't want this to be an occasion for either one of us to spoil Margo's wedding, so I left him alone.

Being one of the last to leave the reception held at the Knights of Columbus Hall, I hugged and kissed Margo goodbye telling her we would write more often. I shook Frank's hand and told him he was a lucky guy. Walking to my car, I took a deep breath of fresh air. It was a moonless night. There were only a few cars left. A light breeze lifted the ends of my hair and brought the smell of smoke. I looked around and saw a man smoking a cigarette as he leaned against a car. With my heart skipping a beat or two, I realized it was Martin. He didn't wave or say anything; he just stood there studying me from afar. Feeling slightly uncomfortable, I slipped into my car, locked the doors, and headed onto the main road towards the motel where I would be staying.

Parking in front of the motel with the pink vacancy light flashing, flashbacks of another bride came to mind. As I gathered my belongings from the car, I spied a small package with my name on it in large capital letters. Tucking it under an arm, I grabbed my purse and overnight bag and headed to my room.

Dropping my bag and purse on the floor, I sat on the edge of the bed and fingered the package. Using the hotel key, I cut the edge of the envelope and dumped the contents on the bed. Staring up at me were photos of Martin and me on our wedding day. There were five of them. Two were taken at The Falls Park where we were married; there was one with my parents and brothers, one with Martin's parents and Margo, and the last one was a picture of me and Martin standing by my Pontiac Tempest decorated with a "just married" sign. I vaguely remembered the photographer my mother had hired, but I had never seen the pictures. They must have been sent to Martin months ago and he had put them into my car at Margo's reception.

I studied them thoughtfully. Martin was not smiling in any of them. In the family pictures his eyes were dark and cold. In the pictures at The Falls Park, Martin was looking off somewhere in the distance. With my arms wrapped around his waist in the "Just Married" picture, Martin stood woodenly with his eyes downcast. Remembering Martin's aloneness at Margo's wedding and his aged appearance, I felt a deep sadness for him even though I did not know this man. I had never known him.

21

The school year ended and I headed to my parent's home for a week. My brother, Zeke and his fiancée were there. Rob had never really left home; he lived down the road a quarter of a mile and helped my dad farm. We enjoyed good food and good conversation and shared the chores that needed to be done. Stephanie, Zeke's fiancée, was energetic, bright and would be a good addition to the family. Since my parents were in their late sixties, I could tell they were aging. They were not as energetic, took their time planning and carrying out things, and seemed to look forward to a daily afternoon nap. I especially noted the change in my mother. She had always been the social planner and cheerleader in our family. The disorganization in a household that had always been neat and tidy when we were all growing up was somewhat disconcerting to me. I wondered what to do about it but then realized making changes would be an invasion of their privacy in a world they had become comfortable with.

The following week, I returned to Adams to get ready for summer break. While taking down bulletin boards, carrying plants to my car, locking files and medical cabinets, my mind ventured back to memories of various students and their predicaments. Eli was foremost in my mind. I wondered if he would take swimming lessons, play on a ball team, attend Bible school, or take a vacation with his dad. Did he have grandparents he would visit? While carrying my last load to the car and with the June heat beating down on the school parking lot, a boy whizzed up on his bike.

"Ms. Christiansen, Ms Christiansen, I was hoping I would see you," an out of breath boy's voice shouted.

I looked up to see Eli, and a warm smile spread across both of our faces.

"Eli! I've missed you already. What are you up to?"

"Well, I never said goodbye and I wanted to…."

"Let's not say 'goodbye.' I'll see you in church, right?"

"Yea, I guess so," Eli looked aside wondering what else to say.

"Are you taking swimming lessons or playing ball? What do you plan to do with your summer, Eli?" I questioned.

"I'm not much into ball. Tried it a couple of times. I love to swim. The guards at the pool call me a pool rat. That's okay; I don't mind."

"So you spend a lot of time at the pool. That's good. Who takes care of you during the day—while your dad is at work?"

"Mrs. Christiansen, I'm going into fifth grade, I don't need a babysitter," he giggled at the thought.

"Probably not," I laughed. "Are you going on vacation?"

"I think so. My grandparents live in Nebraska. Dad said he would take some time off so we could go. I just hope there's a water park along the way."

"Sounds like fun."

And with that, Eli hopped on his bike, turned to give a quick wave and was gone. I stood there feeling very alone. I watched him peddle down the sidewalk past the city park and turn a corner. The parking lot was empty. There was that feeling of nothingness that popped up occasionally—an empty feeling. Brushing it aside, I hopped in my car making a mental list of all I needed to do when I got home. Summer, I should get excited about it.

Driving home, I did some thinking. The Buddha said, "All that we are is the result of what we have thought." Ralph Waldo Emerson said, "What a man thinks of himself, that is which determines or rather, indicates, his fate." Giving up the emotional debris was harder and easier than I first thought. I didn't think about Martin every minute of the day as I used to; however, I did think about the relationship daily. It was just there. When I got up alone in the morning, seeing other couples together, watching families shop together; it just kept coming up. The kind of relationship my parents had and a family with a husband I thought I would have might never materialize for me. I no longer resented Martin; in fact, I felt sorry for him. I simply wished that Martin had happened to someone else instead of to me. Being introspective, however, I kept reminding myself that Buddha and Emerson were right. I would stay positive, find the silver lining, and look for opportunities to have a fulfilling life as a single woman if that was God's wish. *Que sera sera.*

I had eight weeks before school resumed. One rainy morning, I took a pad and pencil and wrote "SUMMER OPPORTUNITIES." While the coffee pot rumbled, I took a quick shower. Dressed in bright colors, I returned to the kitchen and dropped two pieces of rye bread into the toaster. I set out a placemat, chose my favorite mug from the cupboard and filled it to the brim, and lightly covered my rye toast with peanut butter and a little heavier coating of blueberry jam. Enjoying the steamy aroma of Folger's coffee, I eyed the blank pad with its neat capital heading. Picking up the pencil, I started to write: clean out closets, line up box for Good Will, wash and wax cupboards. The blueberry jam kept drawing my attention. I took a large bite of toast, closed my eyes and tasted the wonderful mix of rye, warm peanut butter, and blueberries. With sticky fingers, I crossed out "clean out closets, line up box for Good Will, and wash and wax cupboards." Underneath I wrote: look for new apartment (one with a view), take Mom and Dad on short vacation (fishing), work out, get a new haircut, volunteer at the hospital. Smiling the entire time I finished my breakfast, I washed the dishes and attached the SUMMER OPPORTUNITIES list to the refrigerator door.

That afternoon, I dug out workout clothes, walked downtown to the florist, and bought a daisy bouquet and one single daisy. I walked to the hospital, asked which patient needed a little cheer, and delivered my bouquet to an elderly lady with a recent hip break who had not had family members visit. At first she questioned me, but I left her smiling. The single daisy I took home and placed in a vase in the middle of my kitchen table to remind me life was indeed wonderful, and I would miss out if I didn't throw myself into it with a little more zest than I had in the previous months. Daisies are pretty hardy, but this one lasted longer than expected. Each day it greeted me, and each day I chose to see it as an opportunity to put a little joy in someone's life—which in turn, brought joy back to me. I made a pie and shared it with my apartment neighbors. I called my parents, and we set aside a week to go fishing. I tried to walk everywhere I had to go and felt healthier than I had in months.

While looking at the apartment ads, houses for rent/sale in the local paper, one in particular caught my eye. *Two bedroom house, cottage style, good location, priced to sell. Call owner....* Within fifteen minutes, I had talked to the owner, made an appointment and was out the door. Ted and Peggy met me as I walked up the driveway of their home. I introduced myself as they studied me. As they took me from room to room, I sensed a pride and love for their home—how they had cared for it and the many memories it held. We sat at the kitchen table with iced tea to discuss price, move in date, and the types of papers we would both need to sign. Telling them I would let them know within a week, I left feeling giddy at the possibility of living in this house.

I knew I could afford the down payment and monthly payments. The house was walking distance to school, downtown, the city park, and pool yet was situated in a quiet neighborhood. The home had been lovingly and carefully tended over the years. The shingles and siding had been replaced two years before. The landscaping was attractive but did not require a lot of care. On a corner lot, the house had an all-seasons room built on the backside. From this room, I could see children playing in the park and enjoy the beautiful flowers Ted and Peggy had planted in their back yard. Throughout the house, the carpeting and wall colors were complementary and quiet. During the rest of the day, I contacted my banker, my parents and my brother, Zeke, for advice. As I slipped under the covers that evening, I thought about where I would put my furniture, what would go in the cupboards and planned how to set-up each and every room. I fell asleep asking God to help me make a good decision.

The following Sunday, on a beautiful clear morning, I walked to church dressed in a sundress I had not worn in years, matching handbag, and sandals. My skin was a light tan from all the walking I had been doing outdoors. Pastor Paul greeted me at the door with a "Good morning, great day, nice to have you here," and an usher took me half way up the center aisle before handing me the bulletin. While reading it and listening to the organist play "Beautiful Savior," I felt a light tap on my shoulder. Turning, I saw Eli and his dad.

"Mrs. Christiansen, I didn't think I'd see you already," he hunched his shoulders and snickered.

"Me either. How have you been? Any swimming yet?"

"Sure, every day."

Eli's dad quieted him, and I turned forward.

The sermon title was "Look for God's Way." Pastor Paul cleared his throat, scanned the summer crowd and started:

"In II Kings, we have the narrative of three kings who have joined forces to fight an enemy. On the way to battle they become lost in the wilderness. They run out of water. Everything, and I mean everything, seems to go wrong. They are scared and fear they will soon be destroyed by the enemy." Pastor Paul paused for a drink of water. "One of the kings tries to blame God for their problems....can you imagine that?" Pastor looked over his glasses at his flock before continuing. "One of the other kings, King Jehoshaphat, suggests that what they really need to do is seek the counsel of God's prophet, Elisha. II Kings 3:18 contains Elisha's words of comfort to the three kings-- words that can also be a comfort to us. Elisha said, 'This is but a light thing in the sight of the Lord.'"

Mesmerized by the sermon, I felt another light tap on my shoulder. Turning slightly, I hear Eli's whisper, "Ms. Christiansen, Elisha—that's almost like Eli."

"Eli," his father cautioned. "Sit tight."

Pastor Paul continued, "...What a comfort! That which appears hopeless, that which seems impossible, that which you and I think may never come to pass—it's all 'but a light thing in the sight of the Lord..'"

I heard Eli whisper over and over behind me, "Elisha, Eli, Elisha, Eli, Elisha, Eli," and I had to smile about his sense of humor.

Taking a deep breath, I redirected to Pastor Paul.

"But, then Elisha tells the kings to do something very unusual. He tells them just to go out and dig ditches. I suspect this made no sense to the three kings, but they did it, and God delivered them from destruction."

Pastor Paul took a drink of water, looked over his Sunday morning sheep, and continued. "It was this incident that made me realize that my solution to my problems and God's solution may be completely different. Yes, I must always find God's way—and follow it faithfully. Our biggest problem 'is but a light thing in the sight of the Lord.' And He is able to perform mighty miracles for his glory—and our betterment—if we but seek his will."

Mighty miracles. Seek his will. But a light thing in the sight of the Lord. My solutions? God's solutions. God delivered...

With many thoughts racing through my head, I sang "Beautiful Savior" with the congregation.

"Go in peace and praise the Lord," the pastor stated.

"Thanks be go God," the congregation answered.

As I turned to leave the church, I almost knocked Eli down.

"Eli!"

This time, it was his dad's turn to speak.

"I'm sorry. Ms. Christiansen, is it? Eli isn't usually this noisy in church."

I didn't say anything, but found myself staring at Eli's dad. They resembled each other immensely. The staring embarrassed him and he started to blush.

"Sorry," I gently touched his arm wanting to relieve him, "but, you and Eli, you look so much alike."

"Ummm, he talks about you all the time. I guess this is one kid for whom the summer can't go fast enough."

"Dad…" Eli almost complained. "That's not true. It's just that Ms. Christiansen…"

Before they both became embarrassed, I interrupted Eli.

"Eli, next time you go swimming, let me know. I'd like to come and watch you swim."

"Hey, how about next week, I mean tomorrow, Monday. Will that work?"

"That will work," I ventured after only a moment's thought. "What time?"

"Well, let's see; the pool opens at 1:00." He turned to his dad. "Can I go right after lunch tomorrow?"

Eli's dad seemed to consider it carefully, head down, hand on his chin. He was cleanly shaved, and his fingers were long and well-manicured.

"Sure, Eli, I think that's a good idea."

Pastor Paul interrupted our conversation with "good mornings" all around and asking what we planned to do during vacation. Eli blurted out that he intended to do a lot of swimming. Eli's dad mentioned that in between Eli's pool time, he hoped to get a chance to visit Eli's grandparents. When everyone's attention turned to me, I stuttered around a bit before answering.

"Well, tomorrow, I'm watching Eli swim. After that, I'm not sure."

Pastor Paul shared that he planned a fishing trip to northern Minnesota at a small secluded lake offering cabins, live bait, fishing boats. I immediately became interested and asked him for more details. The fishing trip I had considered for my parents just might become a reality.

Everyone laughed a little and we all headed toward our cars. Before we parted, Eli's dad turned toward me.

"Excuse me, Ms. Christiansen," he extended his hand. "I don't think we've formally met. I'm Eli's dad, Dan."

22

Later in life, I would read from Phillip Gulley's book, *Signs and Wonders*, "There are things we see with our eyes, sitting high and looking out. There are things we see with our hearts, sitting still and looking in." This was the summer I started to see things with my heart. Eli became very precious to me. During the time I spent with my parents on Lake Pimushe, I saw them with different eyes. I walked daily, read the Bible every morning before starting my day, watched Eli swim, and decorated my first home.

A couple of weeks after visiting Ted and Peggy's home, I signed all the proper papers at the bank and was a first-time homeowner. I took possession by the end of June. I started packing my limited personal possessions, took boxes of no-longer used items to Good Will, and organized what was left.

I took my breaks after lunch each day and headed to the pool to watch Eli do the "pool rat" thing. Cannon balling off the board, swimming underwater the width of the pool, reciting the pool rules by heart, he was where he loved to be. One day while sitting on a spectator bench near the deep end, someone came up behind me.

"Hi."

Turning, I saw Eli's father, sack lunch in hand.

"Hi," I answered feeling a little warmer than the summer day.

"Eli said you've been coming almost every day." He smiled before continuing, "I thought I'd better show up."

"He really loves the water, doesn't he?"

"Always has. His mom taught him to swim even before he started private lessons and then, later, group lessons with the guards here at the pool," Dan reflected.

"He'll probably be sitting in the guard chair in a few years—a guard himself. He has all the rules memorized, you know."

"Doesn't surprise me," Dan answered. "Do you care if I join you?"

101

"Please sit down." I shifted towards one end of the bench while Dan took a spot at the other end.

We both soaked up the sun as Eli sauntered toward us a huge grin on his face.

"Dad, what are you doing here?"

"Hey, Eli," he chuckled. "Thought I'd eat lunch and watch you act like a fish."

Eli smiled, waved slightly, and headed towards the diving boards anxious to show off for his dad.

"Have you had lunch?" Dan asked.

"Oh, yes, please eat; you're probably limited for time."

"Yea, a little, but it feels really good to be here." He hesitated before continuing, "You're really good for Eli. I really appreciate you sacrificing your time to be with him."

"Believe me, it's not a sacrifice. This is my break time. It's good for me, too."

"Well, anyway, thank you." I might have mistaken it, but I think he winked at me.

Finishing a bologna sandwich, a Pepsi, and a Little Debbie cookie, he brushed the crumbs from his lap, wadded up his paper lunch sack, and tossed it into the garbage can nearby. As he stood, Eli ran around the corner of the spectator fence with a towel draped over his shoulders, soaked.

"Hey, Dad, are you leaving?"

Dan tousled Eli's wet hair and replied, "Gotta get back to work. Any suggestions for supper?"

"Hmmm." Eli looked at me as if asking for suggestions.

Shrugging my shoulders, I answered, "Hot dogs are always good summer fare."

"Sure, hot dogs, that's it. Hot dogs on the grill. Are you coming Ms. Christiansen?"

"Com... coming?" It came out as a stutter—a bad one.

Dan sensed my embarrassed response.

"Sure, come on over. We'll put an extra hot dog on the grill."

"Well, I'm not sure I...."

"Ms. Christiansen, do you know where I live?" Eli interrupted.

"Yes, but..."

"See you at 6:00." Eli turned to go back into the pool.

I wasn't sure whether this whole scene had been planned by Eli and his dad or if it had just happened spontaneously. Whatever it was, it appeared that I was going to Eli's house for supper. Pondering how all of this had quickly fallen into place, I lifted my head to see Dan staring at me.

"See you at six, then." Giving a thumbs up to Eli and waving, he walked back to his car.

As I approached Eli's home, I smelled hot dogs grilling. Avoiding the front door, I rounded the house to the backyard. Eli and his dad were grilling, setting out chips, paper plates, ketchup, mustard, pickles, the works.

"Smells great," I commented.

"I'm starving," Eli replied.

"You are always starving, son." Turning to me, he smiled, "I think my son has a hollow leg."

I placed a pan of Rice Krispies bars on the table and asked if I could help.

We all soon settled around the table and feasted. I hadn't had hot dogs on the grill for years. Eli lead the conversation by asking what our favorite swim strokes were. Dan shared a few things from work, and I let the cat out of the bag by telling them of my move.

"Moving, where?" Eli almost panicked.

"To a house. I'm in an apartment now. I'll have more room."

"Where?" he persisted.

"It's in town. In fact, it's not far from your house, and it's close to the pool. Real convenient, wouldn't you say?"

"Sure," he started to smile.

Eli's dad only nodded quietly.

"Let me help you clean up," I changed the subject.

Rising from the picnic table, I started to gather the leftovers. With hands full, we all headed toward the back door. Once inside, I couldn't help but notice how clean, neat, and organized Dan and Eli's house was. Eli tapped me on the shoulder and motioned for me to follow him.

"Want to see my room?"

Looking at Dan for permission, he nodded, and I followed Eli.

Eli's room was frugally decorated: light blue walls; blue cotton bedspread; a few books in a bookshelf along with some miniature cars, a piggy bank, an old, somewhat faded teddy bear and pictures; neatly framed pictures of Eli and his mom, Eli and his mom and dad, Eli's dad and mom together. Eli noticed me looking at them.

"That's my mom... and my dad... and me, of course," he informed me.

"I'm sure you miss your mom," I said not knowing the right thing to say.

"Yea. This is my favorite one." It didn't seem to bother him.

He picked up the picture of Eli and his mom and dad. Eli looked to be about six or seven. It was by a stream. It looked strangely familiar to me.

"May I see it?" I asked. Taking it from Eli, I noted the many fingerprints on the glass. Eli had shared this with many others.

"Eli, where was this taken?"

"Lake Isica, or something like that. I could never get it right. It's in Minnesota. We went fishing once and then went to this lake that's the beginning of a big river."

"The Mississippi River."

"Yea, that's it."

I almost jumped realizing that Dan had entered Eli's room quietly and was looking over my shoulder at the picture. The proximity was a little tense but not in a bad way.

"It's Lake Itasca, Eli," Dan quietly stated.

"Well, I was close."

"Yes, you were," I smiled at his innocence and turned so that I was facing them both. "You may not believe this, Eli, but I was at the same spot many years ago with my family. In fact my friend even painted a picture of me by this stream; it was such a special memory."

"Wow. Can I see it?"

"Sure, some day." I needed to change the subject and get out of Eli's small bedroom. Smelling Dan's cologne for some reason was causing me to perspire. "Let's get to the dishes."

"Eli and I can do those Ms. Christiansen," Dan almost whispered as he and Eli followed me out of the bedroom.

"Please, call me Karen, and you can, too, Eli; that is, until school starts."

"Ahhhh, Ms. Christiansen, that's a long ways away."

"Yes, it is. Let's just enjoy summer now." I stopped in the kitchen to pick up my Rice Krispies pan, turned, thanked them both for the hot dogs, and was out the door and on my way home. I didn't know if I had enjoyed the evening or not.

23

Not knowing for sure how to understand what had happened at Dan and Eli's house, I didn't sleep well. At 5 a.m., I decided to get up and take my usual morning walk, but it turned out to be anything but usual.

Leaving the house, I walked to the end of our street and decided to take a different route which would carry me over a bridge and to the other side of town. It felt good to stretch leg muscles and clear my head.

I heard the clink of cans before I saw him. A man dressed in a ragged t-shirt and filthy jeans was going through garbage bins behind an apartment complex. Worth five cents each, I had been told by one of my students that the rich people throw away the cans on purpose so the poor can pick them up and get money for them. I laughed until I remembered his family circumstances, realized he wasn't kidding and quickly changed the subject.

I passed the garbage sorter wondering if I should offer him money or food but realized I'd have to return home to be able to do either. He glanced at me briefly and went on about his work.

A light fog covered the river and enveloped the bridge above it. I enjoyed walking in the fog. Even though a few blocks from home, I felt like I was entering another world. Striding out and taking periodic peeks at the river below rippling over hidden rocks, I soon realized a man was directly in front of me just steps away. His pace slower than mine. Not wanting to spook him, I cleared my throat, quickened my pace and soon was within a couple of feet from his backside. The shirt was plaid—orange, tan and blue—nicely pressed. His dark hair was sticking out beneath a baseball cap.

I passed him quickly not wanting to stare—mumbling a quick "good morning."

He said nothing as he turned his face toward the river.

After another quarter of a mile, I checked my watch and decided to head back. I wanted to get some work done at the school—paperwork I hadn't had a chance to take care of during the school year. A stunning sunrise was doing its best to sneak between the clouds dissipating any suspicions I might have involving early morning strangers.

After a breakfast of oatmeal, packing my lunch, showering, and pulling on comfortable clothes, I did a quick walk-through the house to fluff a pillow, swipe the dust off the television screen and restack yesterday's mail. Pulling the car keys from my handbag and walking out the door, I looked up to see a man walking across the street--in a plaid shirt—orange, tan and blue. A baseball cap covered his head and half his face. I hesitated and thought *new guy in the neighborhood*, but my spine started tingling. Was I being followed? He kept his pace, didn't look up. I watched him turn at the end of the block, and I got in my car and headed toward school; and probably would not have given it another thought if he hadn't shown up later in the day in the place he did.

The school was empty except for the occasional custodian busying himself with room cleaning. The hours passed as I sorted and cleaned files I hadn't been able to get to during the school year. I was literally buried in my work when a knock at my door startled me.

It was Bob, our middle school custodian.

"Sorry, didn't mean to scare you," he offered.

"No problem, Bob. How's your summer going?"

"The usual." And, then, he smiled. "You got a new friend?"

"You mean Eli?" I asked thinking he had seen me at the pool with Eli.

"Oh, no. There's some guy outside the building. He keeps walking around it, trying out a door here and there. We've been having a good time watching him. Haven't seen him before….. you don't have some long lost brother or cousin who might be looking for you, do you?" He quizzed.

I started laughing thinking he was kidding me and then stopped.

"What's he wearing?" I asked.

"A plaid shirt, baseball cap, jeans… can't see his face." Bob replied and noticed my concern.

"Where is he now?" I asked and walked to a window to peek out.

"You know him?"

"No. But he was on my walk this morning and then outside my house."

"Well, that is a little strange. Do you want me to call the cops? Do you feel threatened?" Bob was trying to be helpful, and I didn't know whether to fill threatened or not. Not wanting to make more of something than needed, I thanked him for his concern and told him I would be fine.

After checking my surroundings, I left the building, and before getting into my car, I checked the parking lot and the car itself. Everything seemed to be normal.

I picked up the paper when I got home trying to focus on something else. *Singles Meeting. 6:30 p.m. Potluck at Senior Citizens' Center. Bring a single friend. Help us plan our events for the next six months.*

Sounds interesting, I thought. I called Janet, a single second grade teacher at our school, and asked her if she had ever gone. *No.* Would she care to give it a try? *Maybe.* By the end of the phone conversation, I had decided to bring goulash; Janet had decided to make a German Sweet Chocolate cake. She would pick me up at 6:15.

Feeling somewhat foolish, I dressed in a sundress and sandals and pulled my hair back in a ponytail. Janet arrived in summer slacks and a white sleeveless shirt. Feeling over-dressed, but not having time to change--why didn't we discuss *this* on the phone-- we were some of the first to arrive.

"Main dishes on the left, desserts on the end," a gray haired lady ordered as we arrived.

Coffee was perking nosily in a large pot in a corner; the smell of it relaxed me somewhat. Others arrived. I detected Old Spice, Jean Na'te, and other fragrances along with baked beans, cheesy potatoes, and meatballs. Karen elbowed me.

"I can't believe we're here," she murmured.

"Sorry," I apologized. "I guess it was my idea."

"Only kidding. New experiences are okay. Plus, we'll get a good meal out of this," she chided.

Getting in line with the others, I noted the women outnumbered the men by about two to one. The men were definitely getting a lot of attention. They varied in age from about thirty to seventy-five and came in all sizes and shapes. A couple of them joined Janet and me at our table. Introducing themselves as Marinus and Will, we soon had a lively conversation going. We all went back for seconds and dessert. Before the night was over, we had planned events for the next six months: picnic in the city park, a dance, card playing with prizes, Halloween party, Thanksgiving feast, and a Christmas exchange.

Gathering our empty potluck dishes, Janet and I headed towards the door with Marinus and Will at our heels.

"Want to catch a movie?" Will asked as we headed toward our car.

"It's getting late," I responded while searching the bottom of my purse for car keys.

"No. I mean Friday. There's a show in town. Marinus and I could pick you girls up." Will stopped between my car and me waiting for an answer.

I looked to Janet for help.

"Thank you. You can check some other time. But, this weekend will not work out," and she smiled sweetly. She was better at this than I was.

Later, at my house we replayed the evening's happenings. Marinus and Will were farmers without wives who apparently showed up often at the singles' events looking for companionship. They seemed to be gentlemanly, but I had no interest in seeing either one again. Karen agreed. We wondered if we had missed out on meeting someone more interesting because these two had swamped us with attention from the beginning. We put the picnic in the city park event on our calendars knowing we didn't need to decide tonight whether to participate or not.

A month passed. I busied myself with moving in, doing lawn work, watching Eli swim a couple of times a week, and following my usual summer daily routine of early morning walking and devotions. Dan showed up once at the pool during that time with his lunch to watch Eli swim. It had been a few weeks since our evening with the grilled hot dogs.

"How's your summer going?" I ventured.

Acting almost shy or withdrawn, he raised his eyebrows as if the question had a hidden meaning. "Well, it's going. How about you?"

"I've been busy with the moving and just getting involved with different things."

"Oh."

"How about Eli? He's having a good summer, isn't he?"

"Well, Eli loves the pool. If the town didn't have it, I don't know what he'd do."

We watched Eli play keep-away with a sponge ball with a few friends in the water. Dan got up, threw his paper lunch bag in the trash, and left. Puzzled, I wondered if something was wrong.

Eli burst around the corner.

"Where's my dad?"

"He just left, Eli. He finished his lunch…. and then he left."

"Oh, he's been weird lately."

"What do you mean?" I questioned.

"I don't know. He doesn't say much. I don't think he's mad at me."

"Well, you could ask him, you know. If you really want to know—he might let you know what's bothering him—if anything."

"Sure." And, with that, Eli was off and running home.

Janet and I decided to do the singles picnic in the park thing. With a potato salad and Jell-O-cake, we walked across the park grass in the heat of an early evening in late July. The shelter house was alive with chatter and the organization of food and paper plates and napkins. After dropping off my cake at the dessert end of the table, I turned and was face to face with Dan and the smell of fried chicken.

"Uh, hi," he stammered.

"Hi, I didn't know you went to these things?" I smiled softly and started to touch his arm but pulled away.

"This is my first time. I saw it in the paper. You'll have to fill me in. I'm kind of out of my element, here." He smiled.

"This is just the second time for me and Janet. Do you know Janet? Let me introduce …?"

"Yes, I know Janet. She had Eli in second grade."

At that, Janet interrupted, "Eli's dad. How nice to see you! I didn't know you came to these things…."

"First time." He repeated moving the bucket of chicken from one arm to the other. He kept looking at me.

"Over there," I pointed. "The chicken, you can take it over there."

After a prayer, we all filled our plates and seated ourselves. With my attention focused on Dan and my surprise at his being there, I had not noticed that Marinus and Will were also there. Soon, with filled plates, we were all at one table—all five of us—Marinus, Will, Janet, Dan and me. Dan introduced himself to Marinus and Will. There was conversation about farming and a little about Dan's job. As Marinus and Will tried to give Janet and me attention, I felt Dan studying me. Feeling somewhat awkward, I chose to sit quietly.

"What's the matter, Karen?" Will teased. "Cat got your tongue?"

Wincing at his cliché as it suggested a familiarity that didn't exist, I answered stiffly, "It's a lovely evening. The food is great. I'm just taking it all in."

"Well, there's still time for the late show. That's tonight. What do you think?" Will asked loudly.

Everyone was looking at me. Janet almost choked on her blueberry pie. Marinus was looking back and forth between Janet and me—as if my answer depended on his evening plans with Janet. Dan simply studied me with a look I hadn't seen before.

I looked at Janet—could she save us, again? She simply shrugged and smiled sweetly as if to say, *let's see how you handle this one, Karen?*

At that moment, Dan came to life.

"Karen and Janet are going to the movie with me tonight. Sorry guys."

"Ahh, come on," Marinus threw his napkin down in mock disgust.

"Sorry… had it all planned out before we got here." And with that, Dan rose from the table and walked to the trash barrel. I was speechless. It had taken a lot of nerve.

Looking around and feeling a little giddy at Dan's reaction, I stated, "There's a lot of single women here. I'm sure someone would like to go to the movie tonight."

Janet and I picked up our dishes and excused ourselves. Marinus and Will were making comments like, "Wait till next time…. We don't give up easily…."

Janet took me by the elbow and turned me to face her. "I'm going home in a few minutes. *You're* leaving with Dan. This guy is interested in you."

"What? He asked us both to go to the movies. Besides, he probably wasn't even serious. Eli is at home waiting for him. He probably just saw that we needed an excuse not to go with Marinus and Will."

"Oh, no, you're wrong on this one, Karen. I'm leaving…. Here he comes." She squeezed my hand slightly. "Have a good time. I'll call you tomorrow."

Feeling flustered, I shooed a fly away from the one remaining piece of cake and picked up my pan. Dan was standing next to me with his bucket of take-out chicken with only a thigh left.

"Here, take this cake home to Eli. With the chicken, he'll have enough for lunch tomorrow."

"Thanks. We'll leave it off on the way to the movie," he answered.

"Movie? We don't even know what's playing."

"Then, we'll find out. I haven't been to one in years."

"What about Eli?"

"Eli will be fine. We'll take in the early show and I'll be home by 9."

24

Patton had finally arrived in town. The movie had won an academy award in 1970; George C. Scott had won Best Actor; and Franklin J. Schaffner, best director. The movie was about Patton's life as a general in World War II. *Old Blood and Guts*, Patton's nickname, was given due to his rough speech and toughness.

"What do you think?" Dan asked as we read the marquee while driving past in his car.

"It's a long movie. I'll take a rain check if you don't mind."

I was feeling light-hearted. A movie about a rough and tough general with a world war as a backdrop could spoil my evening.

"O.K.," Dan ventured. "I have another idea."

"Yes?" I had given him an out; apparently, he didn't want it.

"How about a walk? It's cooling off. After all that food, it would do me good."

"Ahhh... me, too. That idea, I like."

We returned to the park where my car was parked. Starting out with the weather, we covered everything from how Eli was doing in school, to Dan's job, my job, our small community, and church activities as we walked around town. Nothing was said about Eli's mother, his first wife. Nothing was said about my first marriage to Martin. Returning to the park to pick up both of our cars, Dan took my hand in his and told me how much he had enjoyed the evening.

"So, you'll do the singles thing again? In August..." I stated thinking of something, anything to say.

"I'm not waiting till August, Karen. I'll call you tomorrow."

"All right." I wanted to say *I'll look forward to that* or *great* or *so glad you came tonight*, but this man had been married to the perfect woman and I was anything but.

I turned, got in my car and gave a slight wave as I drove off—excited, but scared.

Sleeping restlessly, I got out of bed at 5 a.m., pulled on my sweats and a t-shirt and headed out into the early morning air. While giving praise to God for the friends in my life, my family and the early morning stillness, I walked a mile or so before heading home. Filling my coffee percolator with an extra teaspoon of breakfast blend, I plugged in the pot and placed my elbows on the countertop waiting for the pot to start gurgling. I don't know why it gave me such pleasure, but it did. I remember my mother filling an old tin pot with water, placing grounds in a sieve and having to wait for it to boil for just so long on top of the stove. At our church, when I was little, there were only certain ladies who *knew* how to make the coffee. Huge blue and white-speckled pots filled with water were placed over a fire. Also involved were coffee grounds and an egg or two all dumped directly into the large pot. Timing seemed to be important.

The phone ringing brought me out of my daydreaming. It wasn't the sound I had expected.

"Hello."

"Hi, Karen. It's me, Janet."

"Hi, Janet. How are you?"

"How am I? The question is—how are you? Did you go to the movie? What did you talk about? What time did you get home? Did he…"

"Stop!" I chuckled. "We skipped the movie.."

"Skipped?"

"Yes, we skipped the movie and went for a walk."

"Ohhh…" She was waiting to hear more.

"Yes, it was *Patton*. You know, the movie about…"

"Sure, I know. Seen it. Not very romantic. Tell me…"

"Janet, I really have nothing to tell you. We decided against the movie and went for a walk instead. No big deal."

"Well, you know that Eli's dad is considered one of the most eligible bachelors around. It's just that with his wife dying of cancer and all, most of us don't know how to approach him."

"He is very interesting. I've never known anyone like him. We spent some time talking about Eli. I was home before nine."

"Are you sure?"

"Janet, why would I make anything up?" I smiled.

"Well, I said I'd call. Hey, are you going to church? Maybe, I'll see you there." And, with that, she hung up. Her, *well, I said I'd call*, reminded me that Dan had said the very same thing.

It was the Tenth Sunday after Pentecost. The congregation sang *Holy Spirit, Hear Us* as Pastor Paul took his seat at the front of the church.

Holy Spirit, hear us
On this sacred day;
Come to us with blessing
Come to us to stay.

Janet nudged me. I moved over to make a space for her in the pew.

Into Christ baptized
Grant that we may be
Day and night, dear Spirit,
Perfected by thee.

My eyes scanned the congregation for Eli and Dan as Pastor Paul began the service.

"Trusting in the word of life given in baptism, we are gathered in the name of the Father, and of the Son, and of the Holy Spirit."

"Amen," the congregation responded.

They weren't in church, Dan and Eli.

With a first lesson from 1 Kings 3:5-12, and a second lesson from Romans 8:26-39, my mind was miles away or, in my case, blocks away. I was remembering last night's walk as Dan and I wandered the streets of our small town. Thinking about what we had talked about and what we had not talked about.

Pastor Paul interrupted my inattentiveness.

"The mission of the church and each baptized Christian is to serve the reign of God. But what is the reign of God? In today's gospel reading Jesus offers images drawn from ordinary life that reveal something of the reign of God. It is like a tree that becomes a safe and sheltering home, like yeast that penetrates and expands, like a treasured pearl, like a net that gains a great catch. The reign of God is God's steadfast desire to unite the human family, with all its great diversity, in a justice and mercy so great and thoroughly life-giving that people will rejoice...."

Janet nudged me, again. "They're not here."

"Who?" I pretended to not know.

"You know, who."

"Shhh... I'm trying to listen."

After closing with the Lord's Prayer and the benediction, Janet and I left the church. She had dropped the subject of Eli and Dan—perhaps thinking that they would have been in church if Dan had been interested in me after the walk last night. I had to agree.

I dropped on the couch in my new home—the place that had given me so much joy—and felt sorry for myself. The buried anger towards Martin reared its ugly head and one question after another surfaced. Who would want me? A disastrous marriage, a divorce, an assault, a venereal disease. How does one start a new relationship with that kind of baggage? How do you tell someone else who just might be interested in you that kind of stuff? When do you tell? I wanted to curse Martin. I wanted to curse myself.

The church bulletin was still in my hands. Remembering that I had daydreamed through the first and second readings, I opened my Bible to Romans 8:26-39, the second reading for today's service, and read.

"We know that in everything God works for good with those who love him, who are called according to his purpose...For I am sure that neither death, nor life, nor angels, nor principalities, nor things present, nor things to come, nor powers, nor height, nor depth, nor anything else in all creation, will be able to separate us from the love of God in Christ Jesus our Lord."

I read it again. And again. And I knew that I would be okay. I knew that God had a plan for my life. I simply needed to trust. No matter what, God's love was all I needed no matter what my circumstances.

As I was giving praise, the phone rang. It was Dan. Eli was sick. Would I come over?

External otitis. It's what Eli had. He complained of itching and pain in his right ear. There was some discharge. When I tenderly placed my palm against the side of his head, Eli complained that his ear hurt *outside*, too. Recommending to Dan that Eli see a doctor the next day and that he give some children's pain reliever to him, I turned to Eli.

"You, young man, have swimmer's ear."

"What? Is that bad? It must be; it hurts a lot."

"You will feel better after your dad gives you some medicine and after you see a doctor tomorrow."

"Why do I have to go to the doctor? Can't you fix it?" Eli was worried; I could tell. There had probably been a lot of talk about doctors when his mother was ill.

"The doctor will probably give you antibiotic drops to place in your ear to help it get better." Noticing his worried look, I continued, "And, you will want to get better, because until you do, there's no swimming."

Eli's eyes grew wide but he said nothing. The prospect of not being able to swim was discouraging. At this point, however, he only felt like resting and keeping his ear covered with a soft pillow. As Dan was bringing a bottle of medicine and a teaspoon into Eli's bedroom, I prepared to leave.

"Thanks, Karen, I really appreciate your coming over." He smiled. "We didn't make it to church today. He woke up with a fever…" His eyes lingered on mine and he seemed to have something else to say.

"I noticed you weren't there—in church. Make sure he sees a doctor tomorrow. He'll be feeling better soon, but it's best that he stays away from the pool for a few days."

Dan said a quiet good bye and I left.

Entering my house, the phone was ringing.

"Hi. Hello," I answered out of breath.

"Hey, it's me, Will. Probably thought I wouldn't call." My heart sank.

"Oh, hi, Will. I'm right in the middle of something. Can I call you back?"

"Sure, I guess. Got a problem?"

"No, I just walked in the door, someone's sick, and I'll need to get back to you."

"Well, guess that's okay." He was trying to be patient. "My number is 555-1212. Got that?"

"Sure, I'll get back to you. Later today." I hung up feeling unkind and inconsiderate but also knowing I had nothing to say to him. I had no desire to see a movie or anything for that matter with this person. He appeared to be nice. However, there was no chemistry. I didn't want to talk to him then or ever, but I knew out of common courtesy that I would have to return the call. Some time.

Later that day, my mother called. We discussed our up-coming fishing trip to Minnesota on Pimushe Lake. It was a secluded location with a few cabins; the nearest town was ten miles away. It would be good to get away.

25

Only about thirty yards from the lake, the cabins were spaced for privacy. After the long drive, Dad parked the station wagon behind our cabin, and the three of us started to unload our gear: fishing equipment, extra jackets, a small suitcase of clothing for each of us, and a couple of boxes of food items. The cabin supplied dishes, pots and pans, and bedding. The back door of the cabin opened directly into the kitchen—a small area with sink, countertop, gas stove, a mini refrigerator, and a painted table with three chairs shoved up against the wall. With three more steps, we were by the bathroom—complete with toilet and shower. Beyond that was a bedroom/living room with a regular sized bed, a cot, two worn-out chairs, and an old TV. On the other side of the livingroom/bedroom, a door opened onto the shoreline. Opening it, the three of us stood and breathed in the lake air while listening to the waves lap at the shoreline. We saw no one. A crystal blue lake surrounded by towering evergreens appeared before us—almost too beautiful to be true. A fish splashed about in the lake. A flock of birds departed from a distant shoreline. Clouds drifted by. Loons called out. We looked at each other and Mom murmured, "God is good."

Dad broke the spell with, "I'm going fishing. Someone needs to catch supper. Anybody coming with me?"

We spent the week fishing, swimming, walking through the woods, eating freshly fried fish for every evening meal, and playing cards. I'm not sure if the black and white old TV set worked or not; we never gave it a chance. During the evening card playing hours, my parents voiced some of their concerns regarding retirement and moving off the farm, and I shared my feelings of frustration involving Martin and how my poor choices could cost me dearly in the years to come.

"Relationships are sometimes messy, Karen," my mother tried. "Don't let it pull you down. Look at it as an opportunity to know more, to be more understanding. Your intentions were good. You *did* love Martin."

"I thought I did. But, I'm not sure I knew what love was or even is now. How did it all go so wrong?"

"I'm not sure. We may never know the answer. I do know that you are our child; we love you and always will, and we want to see you get through this and be happy."

I wanted to cry; the hurt inside me was so big. Trying not to cry, I swallowed and blinked several times to keep the tears from escaping. I knew my parents loved me unconditionally. They had given me so much: a loving home, a work ethic, and the seeds for faith in a God who I knew would never disappoint me.

"Karen, Dad and I have been praying for you. You're going to get through this. Maybe you would feel better about all of this if you would think about it in a different way." She eyed my dad while choosing her next words.

"You can think about your marriage to Martin as a mistake or you can think about it simply as something that did not turn out the way you had planned. So, you step forward and you go on. Mysterious factors sometimes bring people together. Maybe we will all understand this differently in a few years."

Getting up from the table, I hugged them both. Even though Dad had said nothing, his eyes were tearing. I left the cabin and headed toward the lake. The fishing boat was attached to the dock. Loosening the rope, I stepped in the boat, gripped the oars and rowed into the night.

Working the oars until my arms ached and I could row no more, I dropped anchor. Using the lifejackets and making a soft place to stretch out, I studied my surroundings. The sky appeared forever deep; stars decorated a night sky. Shoreline trees whispered night sounds created by the wind, and the lake was as smooth as black onyx and inviting. Shedding my shoes, socks, and clothing, I dove noiselessly into the deep. Remembering the little girl in aqua shorts wading in a stream at the beginning of the Mississippi River, I thought of the lost innocence.

"Think differently about this, Karen," my mother had said.

While wrapping my mind up in self-centered thinking, seaweed had wrapped itself around my arms and legs as I swam underwater. I could be pulled down to the mud and yuck at the bottom of the lake if I gave in, or I could shed the slimy, green stuff and swim free. I scissor kicked to the surface and released the weeds entangling my ankles with lungs bursting and feeling a little scared.

I wanted to blame Martin and was too often caught up in his convoluted thinking. Except for my parents and Margo, no one really knew my circumstances. Over and over I had to turn this over to God because in my simple-sinner condition, the devil kept pulling me back to ugly, unproductive thoughts.

Floating on my back, I studied the night. Be still and know that I am God. Awesome, beautiful: God's creation. "Look up," Dorcus, my friend from church said. "If we would just keep our eyes looking up, we would be better off." I had to agree.

Remembering the verses from Romans read after last Sunday's church service, I felt better. "For I am sure that neither death, nor life, …..nor things present, nor things to come, nor powers, nor height, nor depth, nor anything else in all creation, will be able to separate us from the love of God in Christ Jesus our Lord."

"Amen; it is so," I said outloud feeling slightly better.

Hearing a fish splatter nearby, I brought my feet down to get an up-close look and started to panic. I had lost my bearings; I had lost the boat. Looking from side to side, I could see the shoreline on both sides. Towering evergreens appeared as monster shadows against a dark sky. Feeling foolish and scared, I imagined myself walking the shoreline naked in the middle of the night looking for our cabin. Dear God, what have I gotten myself into?

Something bumped me softly on the shoulder: my boat. Carefully climbing aboard, I laughed softly. It was good to laugh.

As I approached our dock, I saw an outline of two people standing at the end holding hands. My parents. As the boat bumped dock-side, Dad released Mother's hand and secured the boat to a dock post. Mom helped me out of the boat and squeezed my hand before releasing it. Neither said a thing. They followed me to the house, hand in hand and quietly went to their room. Dropping my damp clothes in a heap on the cabin floor and pulling on some flannel PJs, I slipped under a blanket on the cot—remembering the feel of the water on my skin, the sight of the night, and the love of my parents. All gifts of God.

26

Besides fishing, playing cards, and walking, I read. It was 1972, the year of the bird and the Bible according to *80 Years of Best Sellers* (1895-1975), written by Alice Payne Hackett and James Henry Burke. Richard Bach's *Jonathon Livingston Seagull* and *The Living Bible*, a paraphrase in modern English by Dr. Kenneth N. Taylor, were the two top sellers in fiction and non-fiction.

Two From Galilee, by Marjorie Holmes, and *I'm O.K., You're O.K.*, by Thomas Harris, were also in the top ten list. These were feel-good books read in an atmosphere allowing me to regenerate and gather serenity. I also spent a lot of time thinking about Eli and his father, Dan. What "mysterious factors," as my mother put it, might have brought first Eli and then Dan into my life? Although I had spent a lot of time off and on with Eli during the school year and watching him swim at the pool, I had not spent much time with Dan. He seemed to be a good man, but was he really interested in a relationship or was he just as tentative as I for different reasons?

But, then, Karen's words, "This guy is interested in you," and Dan's words, "I'm not waiting until August, I'll call you tomorrow," kept pestering me. Let me take that back; mosquitoes pester. This was more like the smell of wild flowers in the cabin—lingering in the air—a pleasant reminder of their presence.

After loading the dirty laundry, fishing gear, and fresh fish packed in ice; Mom, Dad, and I left Pimushe and headed home. On our drive home, we learned that burglars were caught breaking into the Democratic Campaign headquarters in the Watergate complex. Although the fishing trip had been relaxing, this news and more returned me quickly to the real world. It was early evening when we arrived at the farm. Brother Rob had taken care of the chores and greeted us with a big grin. I helped unpack and decided to stay the night before heading back to Adams.

After a quick breakfast of toast and boiled egg along with a cup of strong, hot coffee, I put my few belongings into my Pontiac Tempest, and headed to Adams. Although it was a two hour trip, it passed quickly with my head full of memories from the lake. As I drove into Adams, it was apparent there had been heavy rain during the night. Leaves hung limply on trees, the streets were washed clean, and it looked more like early spring than the beginning of August. Carrying a bag of laundry over one shoulder, I dug in my purse for my house key as I took the few steps between garage and house. Finding the key and looking up, I noted that the back door was already opened. Opening the screen door, and looking around, I detected large, muddy footprints on the kitchen floor. Being more curious than careful, I ventured through the kitchen and on to the living room. More muddy footprints on my celery green carpet marked a path leading back to the bedrooms.

"Thud, thud, thud," my heart warned me. Stopping, I quietly dropped my laundry bag and purse on the floor, kept my keys as a weapon and followed the muddy footprints. My bedroom door was open; the extra bedroom's door was not. Checking out the bathroom first, Alfred Hitchcock's shower scene from *Psycho* raced through my mind. Relieved that the shower curtain was already pulled back and finding the room in order, I headed to my room, softly, with baby steps.

I scanned the room but saw no one. Dropping to my knees, I checked under the bed. A few dust bunnies scurried as I flipped the coverlet back. I didn't want to check the closet. The blackened knob was old and a bit wobbly. It always creaked when I used it. If anyone was hiding there, the turning of the knob would alert them. So, I yelled.

"I know you're in there; so just come out. Now!" --an attempt to release fear rather than scare anyone.

I yanked the door open and went through the hangers quickly. Dropping to the floor, I checked the back corners. No one had been there.

Closing the closet door, I turned to inspect the one remaining room and immediately noticed that the door that had been shut was now open. Standing quietly in the doorway, with my heart taking a wild ride, I spotted the tell-tale footprints as I heard the back screen door shut ever so quietly. Turning, I raced to the backdoor stumbling over my laundry bag. Seeing no one, I grabbed the phone and dialed the police number posted by the phone. They were there in minutes, took notes, said there had been no other reports of break-ins, asked how long I had been gone, and whether anything valuable had been taken. One of them left to question neighbors to find out if they had seen anyone suspicious in our neighborhood.

Within an hour the police left, and I was alone with muddy foot prints, dirty laundry, and a sense of being violated. Had everything been touched in my house by this stranger? Who would come in the light of day, what did he find, what did he want? Carefully going through my things, I could find nothing missing. Calling Janet, I asked if I could spend the night. It was not likely this person would return, but I was terrified. Janet graciously took me in that night and the rest of the week.

During that week I ventured back to the pool. Eli spotted me and ran over.

"Ms. Christiansen, where have you been?"

"Hi, Eli, your ear must be better."

"Oh, yea. Where were you? My dad and I...."

"I went fishing—with my parents—in Minnesota," I interrupted.

"Oh," he seemed to be thinking. "Why didn't you tell us?"

"I'm not sure. Did you need to know?" Eli's frankness made me smile. He was shivering; it was a cooler day than normal.

"No, I guess not. We just wondered. My dad, he got a little worried."

"Your dad?"

"Yea, he just wanted to be sure you were okay."

"I'm just fine. We caught lots of fish. When do you visit your grandparents?"

"Tomorrow, we're leaving. I'll let Dad know you're okay," and with that he was off. I wasn't okay, but it wasn't Eli's or Dan's problem.

When Sunday arrived, Janet and I rose early, walked together, had our morning coffee, showered, and decided to attend church. Attendance was low with members getting in end-of-the summer vacation time. Pastor Paul started with announcements: "baptized today....., garden table available...., congratulations to Sandy and Scott Lennox on their twenty-fifth wedding anniversary."

My attention was riveted on the pulpit when Pastor Paul started his sermon with, "A lover might say, 'I'd give anything to know that my beloved loves me.'" Looking around, I spotted older couples, younger couples with children, and the widows and widowers who often sat together.

"Deep in the yearning of every human being is a longing to know that at the heart of the universe is a great and good being who loves us. The gospel is that assurance......Our lovers, finding their love reciprocated and settling back in married happiness, may take their joy for granted and forget its immeasurable blessing. This happens often in our lives with God. Unless the ministry of Word and sacraments continues to stir us, we could lose the wonder of being loved and live as if we had no God and no eternal kingdom."

The Lennoxes sat in front of us. With his arm gently placed across her shoulders, they looked as one. A mother to my left cradled a sleeping child. A father across the aisle turned the pages of a picture book while listening to the sermon with a child settled on his lap.

Pastor Paul's words and being in fellowship with other Christians started me thinking. My summer had been off to a good start. I was putting others before myself, and spending time in daily devotions and prayer. The intruder in my house incident had scared me, and I had turned the focus on me. Whether I married or not, I knew I would turn bitter if I only focused on myself. It would be easy to slip into the habit of waiting for someone to be my lover, my protector, my companion for life. Whether I married or not, I could be loveable, and I could care for and love others.

Pastor Paul continued, "When we have the treasure in our hearts, we have an urgent desire to share it with others.… The world is full of people who know no overarching purpose for living, people who have lost their way and wander in a moral wilderness, people whose lives are weighed down with fear and anxiety, people who are lonely and bored, people who carry unresolved guilt."

It's interesting how the devil uses whatever he can to work his way into our lives. While making notes on my church bulletin of what I needed to do when I returned home, Janet nudged me. "What are you doing?" she asked not so quietly. Sometimes Janet acted more like the elementary students she taught than a grown woman.

"Making a list," I whispered back.

"About what?" she snooped.

"Tell you later."

Pastor Paul concluded, "To be captured by the gospel is to be turned around to others. … it is not something we hoard. It is the treasure we give to others."

Admiring the baptismal baby and congratulating the Lennoxes on their twenty-fifth wedding anniversary on our way out, Janet nudged me, again.

"So, the list. Tell me about it."

"I need to go home, *today*. I've been gone long enough. Everything seems to be all right. I can't stay with you forever."

"The list?"

"Oh. It's what I need to do… when I get home… establish a routine again. You know, it's only a couple of weeks before school starts."

After gathering the few items I had quickly put together to be able to stay at Janet's, she drove me home. We had gone back during the week together to clean the carpet, pick up the mail, and make sure no one else had broken in. The police had not come up with anything, and I had not either—nothing seemed to be missing.

About two blocks from my home, I saw him. His back was to us. With hands in his pants pockets, he slowly walked, somewhat methodically—as if trying to miss the cracks in the sidewalks.

"Janet, follow that guy."

"Who?" Seeing him, "Why?"

"Just do it, please," I asked her and then feeling like a child, I slid down the seat until my knees hit the dashboard.

"What are you doing?" she laughed.

"This is not funny. I don't want to be seen. Have you caught up with him yet?"

"Who? The guy who's walking funny? Yea. What about him?"

"Try to see his face. I want you to describe him. But don't act like you're trying to check him out."

"You're starting to scare me."

"Just do it."

"Okay." Janet was starting to sound nervous.

"You're going too slow. He'll know we're looking at him."

"Okay, okay," she stepped on the gas which more than likely brought attention to her car.

"Do you recognize him?"

"No. Never seen him before."

She put on her blinkers, turned the block, and looked back over her shoulder.

"I think this guy used to be good-looking," she tried to describe him. "He looks a little worn out. Looks like he used to have a nice build—a little overweight. Curly hair with an odd streak of gray in the back. Ooooh—he's looking. Dark eyes. We're out of here."

"Martin." I whispered.

"Martin? Martin, who?"

"My husband."

"You're married?"

"X-husband."

"Oh. I didn't know." Her shoulders slumped as if it were her burden.

"I haven't told anyone. Huge mistake--that kind of thing."

"Sorry. No wonder you're different—about men—that is."

I could have questioned her about that one, but my mind quickly went to something else: the man in the plaid shirt on the bridge and, later on that day, outside of the school. How could I have not realized this was Martin?

"Take me home!"

Dashing into my house and sprinting to the back bedroom with Janet following, I went immediately to the drawer where I stored my photo albums and miscellaneous photographs. The wedding pictures that Martin had presumably left on my car seat during Margo's wedding reception were gone.

"What are you doing?" Janet questioned as she looked over my shoulder. "What's wrong?"

"It's Martin. He's been here."

"You'll need to tell me more than that." She added.

"Later. I'll explain everything." I hugged her quickly and left to make a phone call.

Calling the police, I explained what I had discovered. They asked if I wanted to file a restraining order and if this man was dangerous. Restraining order—yes, what did that involve? Was he dangerous? I didn't think so. But, I had never understood Martin, so maybe he was.

27

The sign above the table read "REGISTRATION." Dressed in practical shoes and a professional skirt and jacket, I sat at a table handing out health forms for the upcoming school year. It was late August and the beginning of my second year as the school nurse for the Adams Community School District. Last year I had been uncomfortable on this day—not knowing anyone, not knowing for sure what to do or how to prepare for this job. This year, I knew everyone on staff and many of the students and their parents. But, I was uncomfortable; the discomfort was physical as well as mental. Sores in my pelvic area had returned despite the fact that I was still on the antiviral medication. My lymph nodes were slightly enlarged and walking was painful. Although I had been fortunate the symptoms did not display themselves on my hands and face, I still felt like a walking leper. I had been fortunate by not having an outbreak since being diagnosed. Perhaps the stress of the break-in and school starting had brought it on.

A little girl with a familiar voice broke in. "Hi, Ms. Christiansen, nice to see you; remember me?"

"Liddie Meyers-Jenkins, how could I forget you?" I smiled at her and sat on a chair to get to her eye level. "How was your summer?"

She looked away. "Look, Ms. Christiansen, the leaves are turning colors on that tree outside your window."

"And, so they are. It's time for us to get back to work. Are you ready?"

"I like school. This is a good place for me to be," she smiled and stepped closer.

Pulling her to me, I sheltered her with one arm and brushed her hair back with my other hand. She snuggled against my shoulder briefly, stepped back, and skipped out of the room. I recalled what Cheryl, the school secretary, had said last year at this very time about Liddie —"interesting.

Myself, I think she's a bit of a mystery. She's cute, bright, and, yet, something is missing with that child. She'll be in to see you often."

I had seen Liddie often; however, they were very brief encounters. She had her share of tummy aches, toothaches, hangnails; but she never really expected me to fix anything—just wanted to tell me and then be gone.

Gathering my posters and thumbtacks, I stepped back to scan the room. Did everything need to go in the same place? Should I reorganize for a different look? While reflecting, someone burst into the room.

"Hey, need some help? We made it back."

Turning to see Eli I wanted to hug him. I had missed him. Dropping the thumbtacks and posters, I took him by the shoulders.

"Hey, nice to see you. How was your visit to Grandma and Grandpa's?"

"Great. Dad said they spoil me, but I don't mind it."

"I've heard that is what grandparents are supposed to do."

Eli looked around. "Need some help? Dad's registering me, so I can help out for a while."

"Sure, Eli. Help me decide where these posters should go. You choose a spot; I'll stick the tacks in."

As we were hanging posters, quiet, heavier footsteps entered the room. Nothing was said. I turned to see Dan. I had forgotten how handsome he was. If it's possible to feel warm and fuzzy and nervous and awkward at the same time, those were my feelings. Eli looked from one of us to the other and finally broke the silence with a response only a child could come up with.

"Say something," he blurted looking at both of us.

"Hi," we acknowledged each other at the same time.

"I came to register Eli," he stated the obvious.

"How was your trip?"

"Good. It was a nice get-away. I guess we both needed it. A lot of time on the road, but it was worth it."

"Great. And, now school starts. Summer. What happened to it?" I was searching for topics.

"I'm not sure I know. It didn't exactly go as planned."

Thinking something bad had happened that I was not aware of, I sympathized, "Oh, I'm sorry. What happened?"

"Nothing," Dan tried, and somewhat hesitant, he went on, "I mean, it's nothing. Some of our plans didn't work out. But, we're not giving up, right, Eli?"

A few moments of silence followed. There seemed to be some unspoken communication between Eli and his father.

"Eli was going to help me with the posters, but we can do it .....,"

"No, go ahead Eli; I want to introduce myself to a couple of your teachers. I'll be back in a few minutes. You go ahead and help Karen—I mean, Ms. Christiansen."

Dan returned in a few moments to pick up Eli. The posters had been randomly tacked to the walls—Eli's choice. The plants I had brought were returned to their window spaces.

"Eli, your reading teacher from last year wants to say hi. Remember where her room is?" Dan asked his son.

"Sure," Eli was on his way—the social bug that he was.

Dan closed the door to the nurse's office and took a few steps until we were face to face. He smiled gently. He was tanner and looked rested but his eyes were troubled.

"I need to talk to you. I want to do this in person, and I want to do it without Eli."

Thinking it to be about Eli, furrowing my brow, I encouraged, "Please sit down."

We both sat in the only available chairs—knee to knee—almost touching.

"I've wanted to spend more time with you, get to know you better, that kind of thing all summer, but the opportunity just never seemed to present itself."

Not expecting this, I simply waited for him to continue.

"I guess I'm not much good at this. Eli's mom and I were married for eight years, so I'm a little out of the dating scene. I'm several years older than you are. I have a son. You're not seeing anyone are you?" It all came gushing out.

"No." I kept looking at him. Although I had thoughts of it, daydreamed about it, I couldn't believe that Dan was actually saying these things.

"Good. I'm glad you're not seeing anyone." He seemed to relax.

"No. I'm not." I smiled wanting to put him at ease.

"Good." It was his turn to smile. "Can I call you in a few days?"

"Yes. It gets pretty busy with school starting, but a call would be nice."

"OK. That's where we'll start."

Eli opened the door without knocking and let his dad know he was ready to go--eager to get to the pool before it closed for the afternoon.

Leaving the school that day I had conflicting emotions. I was elated that Dan wanted to spend time with me, but I wondered if he would ever want to have a relationship with someone who had a venereal disease. From there, the worry mounted. We both had past relationships. He had been married to a beautiful woman, the mother of his child, an active member of this community. She died. Dan and Eli still loved and cherished her. I had failed at marriage. I had a disease I had to live with the rest of my life, a disease with a stigma. Could I even have children without risk involved? Then, there was Martin who seemed to just come out of the woodwork every once in a while to make life difficult, and perhaps, threatening. Could I subject Dan and Eli to any of this?

Instead of driving home, I went to church. It was a Wednesday afternoon in August; the secretary was sequestered in her air conditioned office. Entering the unlit, quiet sanctuary, I heard the organist practicing for Sunday's service, *Nearer My God to Thee*. Sitting in the front pew, she noticed me.

"Would you like some privacy? I can stop playing?" She asked.

"No, please play. It's beautiful," I answered.

The words came back. Second verse: *Tho' like the wanderer, the sun gone down; darkness be over me, my rest a stone. Yet in my dreams I'd be, nearer my God, to Thee, nearer my God, to Thee, nearer to Thee.* As she continued to play, I began to pray.

Dear God, forgive me for my sin, mortal that I am. I know not your plan for my life. I'm often confused and misled. I do know that you are my savior and that you gave your life so that I might live in eternal glory with you in heaven. And, that you do have a plan for me. Help me to focus on you and your desires for me; help me to trust. Thank you for your many blessings. To God be the glory in all things…

To the tune of *Nearer My God to Thee*, I left the church refreshed and thankful. On the way home, I picked up ingredients for pizza. As I was throwing together a crust and organizing the cheeses, pepperoni and sauce, the phone rang. Wiping my hands on a dish towel, I answered.

"Hi, it's me, Dan."

"Hi, Dan." I expected his call but not this soon.

"I thought with school starting, I didn't want to put this off. Can I come over?"

"When?"

"Now, is that okay?"

"Sure. Have you eaten? I'm putting together a pizza."

"Sounds good. Eli's making a grilled cheese sandwich. I'll be over in a few minutes." He hung up.

Before I could finish the pizza, he was at the door, a smile on his face and two sodas in hand.

"Wow, you're fast," I said.

"Want some help?" he asked as he placed the sodas in the refrigerator and started opening the pepperoni package.

As the pizza baked, we talked. As we ate the pizza, we talked. While doing the dishes, we talked. Starting out with our growing up years, our parents, our siblings, a little about high school, we eventually covered where we attended college and our first jobs, and then our marriages. We talked about the baggage or issues that we each brought to any relationship. Dan did not seem shocked or repulsed at anything I told him. Sharing with him that I had gone to church after leaving school because of my concerns, he took my hands in both of his, closed his eyes and bowed his head. He offered a simple prayer asking God for guidance. We both said "Amen."

As he stood to leave, he pulled me into his arms and embraced me lovingly. We held each other and for the first time that evening neither of us had anything to say.

28

The school year was a blur. After some initial teasing from fellow faculty members, the community soon viewed us as a couple or a three-some with Eli often in the middle of everything. Homecoming, Halloween, Thanksgiving (his parents, my parents), Christmas (my parents, his parents), New Years, Valentine's Day, the first day of spring, an FFA breakfast, end of the year reports. We talked of marriage but knew it would take work. With the blending of families, with past issues, and knowing that marriage meant a life commitment, we chose not to hesitate but rather to consider the possibilities.

Zeke, my brother, got married. My parents started thinking about moving off the farm so Josh could have a place, as they put it. Margo called and I shared the news. Janet continued the monthly singles' meetings and started dating Marinus. Martin appeared on my doorstep on two occasions, but wandered off on his own. Liddie continued to be my constant in the nurse's office along with a few other students. So much was happening, yet it felt as if the world revolved around us.

Being in love with Dan was like nothing I had experienced. He was my friend. I trusted him. He cared. He valued and appreciated me especially when it came to Eli, the time I spent with him and how I could love him as my own son. We shared our ups and downs. I felt warm and secure. I respected, honored him and had never experienced anything so intimate. I could never replace Eli's mom nor did I intend to. She was a beautiful Christian woman, a loving mother—and they would always have these memories. I was simply and humbly someone else who was to be a part of their lives at this point in time.

29

All of you are in Christ's body, and each one is a part of it. In the church, God has put all in place: in the first place apostles, in the second place prophets, and in the third place teachers; then those who perform miracles, followed by those who are given the power to heal or to help others or to direct them or to speak in strange tongues. They are not all apostles or prophets or teachers. Not everyone has the power to work miracles or to heal diseases or to speak in tongues or to explain what is said. Set your hearts, then, on the more important gifts.

It was one year after our pizza date, as Dan and I lovingly called it, and with a few friends and family members, we were all gathered in our church. Dressed in a flutter-sleeve, empire waist, tea-length, light pink dress and matching shoes, I felt like Cinderella at the ball. I carried a single red rose. Standing at the front of the church before Pastor Paul, Eli and Dan both wore tuxedoes—a decision they both were enthusiastic about. Janet, my maid of honor, stood to my left in a flowered, softly colored sundress.

I turned slightly to see my mom, dad, Rob, and Zeke and his wife, Stephanie, sitting in the first pew. Mom winked as Dad placed his arm around her shoulders. Dan's parents and family were seated on the opposite side.

Again, I faced Pastor Paul. What was this message about apostles, prophets, and teachers? Dan and I were getting married. I focused on our pastor as he continued.

"Set your hearts, then, on the more important gifts," he repeated as if to regain my attention.

Best of all is the following way. I may be able to speak in the languages of men and even angels, but if I have no love, my speech is no more than a noisy gong or a clanging bell. I may have the gift of inspired preaching; I may have all knowledge and understand all secrets; I may have all the faith needed to move mountains—but if I have no love, I am nothing....

Love is patient and kind; it is not jealous or conceited or proud; love is not ill-mannered or selfish or irritable; love does not keep a record of wrongs; love is not happy with evil, but is happy with the truth. Love never gives up, and its faith, hope, and patience never fail.

Love is eternal.

I looked at Dan. He squeezed my finger tips and gently rubbed the top of my hand with his thumb. Pastor Paul continued.

"Those verses from I Corinthians 12 and 13, I have chosen for you today as you commit yourselves to each other before God, your family, and a few friends. I am especially honored, Karen and Dan, that you have chosen me to officiate at your wedding."

I squeezed Dan's hand as Pastor Paul gave a brief message and we recited our vows. After pronouncing us husband and wife, he requested that the few guests come up to the altar with the wedding party as we prayed asking for God's blessings and thanking him for his everlasting love. We ended with the Lord's Prayer and then Pastor Paul handed out hymnals to all of us and asked us to turn to "Blest Be the Tie That Binds."

Our small group sang, *Blest be the tie that binds—our hearts in Christian love, the fellowship of kindred minds is like to that above. Before our Father's throne, We pour our ardent prayers; our fears, our hopes, our aims, are one, our comforts and our cares.*

I didn't sing the last verse. Simply listening with a lump in my throat, I realized something about Dan I had not noted before—his beautiful voice. I turned to look at him. There were so many things we had to discover about one another, and we had a lifetime to do it. He turned to look at me as he finished the song he knew by heart.

After a light supper in the fellowship hall and convincing Eli that he could give up the tuxedo, he left with his grandparents. We hugged and kissed our families a farewell as they all left for their respective homes. Janet packed up the few gifts in her car, gave me a quick hug, and said, "See you in a couple of weeks."

Pastor Paul congratulated us one more time, looked at his watch, and said his wife was expecting him at home. We heard the large church door close behind him. Dan and I were completely alone in the reception area of the church. He took me by the hand, and silently we walked back into the church and sat in the front pew staring at the huge cross in the sanctuary. Pastor Paul had turned off the lights, but a small candle burned brightly on the altar.

"This is where we start our lives as a married couple, Karen. I feel so loved by you, God, and my family right now that I don't know if I want to leave. I don't want to lose whatever we have right now."

Bringing his hand to my lips, I gently kissed the back of it. Because this moment seemed so preciously intimate didn't mean life would be filled with joy and be free of misery. Not knowing how to respond, we sat quietly—shoulder to shoulder, my hand in his. Soon the words came—words I had not prepared.

"Dan… we love each other. We are committed to each other. We don't know what tomorrow will bring, or next week, or next year; but we do know that God is our Savior and King. He has a place for us in Heaven. Knowing that, we can find joy in every day."

Fingering the wedding band he had earlier placed on my ring finger, he hugged me. "I guess that's what drew me to this particular ring," he smiled and gently removed it from my finger. "It's called an 'eternity ring.' Can you see what's written inside the band?"

Taking it from his palm and bringing it closer, I read, "I love you" inscribed on the inside.

Taking the ring from me, he gently slid it back on my finger. There were two small diamonds on a yellow gold band with a larger diamond in the middle. I had assumed it was simply the ring design.

"This ring—it fits what Pastor Paul read from I Corinthians 13: 13. Faith, hope, love—the greatest being love."

I could only gaze at this man and wonder what luck had brought him to me. Thinking "praise be to God" and smiling, Dan and I were suddenly startled by a loud thump in the back of the now darkened church. Turning, we saw no one. Grabbing hands, we hurried out into the twilight of an August evening, jumped into Dan's car and headed out of town. Dan knew our destination, a surprise he had planned. I was in suspense.

I awoke to the sound of crickets chirping and the smell of earth, water, and things growing. Blinking my eyes to get used to the overhead car light, and noticing that Dan was no longer in the driver's seat, I wondered where he was. Stepping out into the night, I quietly closed the door and took a deep breath. I was surrounded by trees, vines, grasses, and the sound of water running. I wondered how long I had slept and where was Dan?

"Karen?" he whispered my name not wanting to scare me. I turned and he gently wrapped me in his arms and chased away the cool night air.

"Where were you? And, where are we? How long did I sleep?'

He laughed. "Which question do you want me to answer? You slept a couple of hours." Taking my hand, he added, "And, if you follow me, that will answer your first two questions." Squeezing my hand, he whispered mysteriously, "I'd ask you to close your eyes, but I don't think that would be safe."

I looked around trying to take in everything, but it was so dark.

"Where are we?" I asked again.

"It's where we're staying. I hope you like it," he almost winced. "It's not your typical honeymoon suite. But I think I know a little bit about you and, well, I'm just hoping you really like it."

"Dan, I'm confused —are we camping here?"

"No, just follow me. Trust me."

Hand in hand, feeling like Hansel and Gretel lost in the forest, I carefully followed him down a set of wooden steps. The further we descended, the stronger the smell became—river water. Soon I could hear it lapping the shore with night time caresses.

"Dan, what is this?" I was mesmerized. Lifting me in his arms, he took the final steps down the dock. After a few steps, the evening clouds parted and a full moon lit our honeymoon suite—a Mississippi boathouse.

Dan retrieved a key from his pocket, opened the door and swooped me off my feet. Carrying me over the threshold, he placed me carefully inside the door and began to fumble his way around. Soon a hurricane lamp was lit, and we viewed our surroundings. A 20 x 15 foot room had everything we needed: cook stove, open cupboards stocked with food, small refrigerator, regular sized bed layered with quilts, desk with an oil lamp, comfortable looking couch, closet space, a small shower-bathroom in one corner, and another corner filled with fishing and boat gear. A large, multi-colored, woven rug covered the middle of the floor, and several pictures of various wild flowers decorated the walls.

"Dan...," I was amazed. How did he arrange all this?

"You don't like it, do you?"

"I'm overwhelmed. How did you do this? Who does this belong to? You know how I love the water." It came out all at once. I hugged him; it was perfect.

"It belongs to a college buddy of mine. It's his wedding gift to us. Someday, you'll meet him. But for a couple of weeks, this will be our home. If you get tired of it, we'll head home earlier..." I shut him up with a kiss and an embrace that left him speechless.

Listening to the water lap at the dock, a riverboat blast from afar, and an ancient clock ticking away in the corner, I couldn't imagine a more perfect place for us. Opening a bottle of Nauvoo wine, slicing some dark brown bread, and setting out some blue cheese, Dan and I sat down for a late night snack. A few minutes later, we dropped our clothes on the floor, crawled under the layers of quilts and spent our first night together on the river.

We spent the next week fishing, boating, hiking, visiting museums, and digging around in old antique shops. Trying new restaurants—tasting everything from fried oysters to jambalaya and more--our taste buds ventured into unknown territory. During our many hikes and boat rides, we enjoyed bird watching-- mockingbirds, redwing blackbirds, robins, ruby-throated hummingbirds, purple martins, and an occasional heron. We swam when we felt like it during the heat of the day or in the middle of the night and went to sleep with the smell of nature ever present in the boathouse.

One day, we rented a canoe, and with a picnic lunch packed in a basket, we paddled a quiet portion of the river. With the sun warming our backs, we paddled close to the shoreline and discovered plants and animal life we had not noticed previously. As we were returning to our start-up spot, a storm arose seemingly out of nowhere and drenched us. As the rain gently persisted, I shared the story of my great grandmother, Fannie, the Indian maiden, who had followed her lover to California and the Gold Rush who, after much heartache, had returned to her family and this very river. Spellbound by the story, Dan tenderly touched my face and ran his fingers through my wet hair. "I always knew there was something unique about you. What a fascinating story, Karen."

Not caring for the night life, we spent our nights at home, in our boathouse, reading to each other, playing gin rummy, and listening to night sounds. The primitively built bookcase held only a few books, but they were worthy. Choosing a college English literature textbook one night, published in 1949, we read Thomas Moore's poems to each other. His sentimental verses, "Believe Me, If All Those Endearing Young Charms" and "'Tis the Last rose of Summer," entertained us. I giggled as Dan stood before me reading just to me. Soon, we were both giggling, tenderly holding each other under the quilts as the river gently rocked our little house.

Memory is a funny thing. As our little house boat bobbled about in the water, I was reminded of another poem from my college years written by Rod

McKuen. After attending a Glenn Yarbrough concert during college years, Margo and I bought McKuen's books and memorized a particular poem.

I have no special bed.
I give myself to those who offer love.
Can it be wrong?
Lonely rivers going to the sea give themselves to many brooks in passing.
So it is with me
undiscovered and alone...

Remembering it, I started crying. Margo and I were not promiscuous; however, we understood the loneliness seeping through the lines. I cried because during this moment in time, I felt immensely blessed. The thing I had feared-- having no one in my life—was behind me. Dan held me closer, and after a few moments asked, "Do you want to talk?"

"No," I answered softly. With crickets' chirping, an occasional owl hooting, and the sound of soft waves against the boat, I fell asleep in Dan's arms—cheek to cheek, my leg wrapped around his, his heart beating with mine.

Monday blended into Tuesday, Tuesday into Wednesday, and so the week passed. Part of the plan was to have Eli join us the second week. With a duffel bag and dressed in his swimming trunks with a towel slung over his shoulder, he arrived noisily with his grandparents more than a few steps behind.

"Hey, look at this! Wow! I can't believe it. I get to stay here?"

Dan and I greeted him with open arms and welcomed everyone in for a boathouse lunch. After a leisurely afternoon with Eli's grandpa and grandma followed by hugs and kisses, they ascended the many steps to reach their car.

As they waved their goodbyes from the top steps, Eli turned to us and asked, "When do we start?"

"Start? Start what?" Dan knew his son well and was only playing games.

"Dad, you know—fishing, swimming—all that good stuff."

"Eli, would you like to go for a boat ride?"

"Sure, Dad, is this boat really ours?"

"Well, it's ours to use during the week. It belongs to the boathouse."

"Sure, let's go."

"Let's all go for a ride. Karen and I will show you around. While we're doing that—we'll plan the rest of the week. How does that sound, son?"

Eli was the first one in the boat.

30

The Mississippi River begins in northern Minnesota and runs its course to the Gulf of Mexico continuously on the move through many states and geographical landmarks. It changes character as it flows—out of necessity—just as we all individually evolved. Human development depends on many things—genetics, environment, the people we know, the places we go and the experiences we have. And so, as time passed, things happened, and we all changed.

I gave up my little house to a retired couple who were just as delighted to have it as I was months ago. I moved into Dan's and Eli's house and a routine developed: school, work, and play.

After five years of marriage, Dan and I were more in love than I had ever imagined was possible. However, it was not the kind of love I had dreamed or expected. It was deeper, more intimate. The feeling of family was a connection that was tangible, like an additional vital organ.

Eli grew to be taller than Dan. His voice at first squeaked but eventually it deepened into a voice much like his father's. When he was in high school, our supper time discussions sometimes revolved around college and career choices. Dan and I had spent several years attending middle school and high school athletic competitions, concerts, and plays. Eli's grades were mediocre; however, he thrived on the extra-curricular activities. This was a contradiction to his grade school years when he seemed to be more comfortable alone; Dan and I both delighted in this change. He volunteered for the stage crew for the spring and fall plans, played the drums, and participated in athletics. Although he often sat on the bench at basketball games or stood with the lineup beside the football field, he felt that he was as much a part of the team as any starter. On weekday nights, we sat around the table discussing our days and then would often retreat to the living room to watch Happy Days or the Rockford Files as a family.

Besides school and family responsibilities and activities, a group of us at school started a birthday club. It was a small group: Pam, a second grade teacher; Cheryl, the office secretary; Barb, a sixth grade teacher; Jeanne, a middle school math teacher; and Heidi who worked with the pre-school children. Enjoying a meal, recognizing the birthday, and appreciating our friendships gave us reason to celebrate once a month. As the years went by, the value of these friendships grew.

Each summer, Dan, Eli, and I returned to the Mississippi River boathouse for our family vacation. After that first summer in the boathouse, Eli starting calling me Karen. Before school started, it was Kare-mom. And soon it was Mom. He asked if I cared; I told him I would be honored.

I continued with my job as the school nurse. Eli often stopped for lunch money, just to say, "Hi, Mom," or ask for advice. I never minded. Liddie showed up almost as often as Eli, and I learned something I wished were not true. She had been sexually abused as a child by an uncle. I ached for her. Attempting to be her mentor, her confidant, I encouraged her not to play the victim's role—but, instead, to decide what she wanted to do with her life, and, then, to let nothing stop her. She wanted to be a nurse.

Dan advanced with the insurance company to a management position. His salary doubled, and we started to dream about the possibilities of buying a lot on the river. Some day, we said. Some day.

My parents moved off the farm; Rob married the new teacher in town, and Zeke and Stephanie moved to Philadelphia and were expecting a baby.

Margo called several times a year. She was expecting their second child and had quit teaching to become a full-time mom. Martin? No one knew his whereabouts. The family was concerned but also assumed that no news was good news when it came to Martin.

As a family, we were active in the church. Eli was confirmed after his ninth grade year. Dan and I were active in adult Bible study groups. Pastor Paul left for another congregation and was sorely missed; however, a new minister with different gifts took his place. To God be the glory. Dan was on the property board; I was on the worship board; Eli was involved with the youth group.

Because I worked for the school district, summers were somewhat leisurely for our family. Eli started working at the pool after passing his Water Safety Instructor course. During his off-times, he helped me with various chores. Dan tried to get off early at least once a week so that we could enjoy a picnic in the park, community theater, or a drive to a nearby lake. Federal and state guidelines were always changing, so I could always use some of my time in preparation for the coming school year.

Even though we all read and discussed the daily newspaper headlines over breakfast in the morning—the Volkswagen Beetle stopped production, first test-tube baby was born in England, cult leader Jim Jones instructed 400 members of his church to commit suicide, and more-- we felt in our hearts that the truly important news was that we were a family. I sometimes heard the neighbors complain about teenage children or husbands and knew that in this respect, I was blessed. I could go to bed each night, consider my daily routine and experiences, and sleep in peace.

After Eli graduated and left for college, Dan and I experienced the empty nest. Someone was missing. I not only missed interacting with Eli, but I missed Eli interacting with his Dad. I viewed school life differently as we no longer had his activities to look forward to. His activities had pretty much become our social life. We talked on the phone a couple of times a week, and he spent a weekend with us as often as he could, but things were not the same. After several months of thinking the house was too quiet, we grew accustomed to it. Thinking about new ways to fill our time, Dan and I checked out the adult education classes in our community and decided to take a class together: German Cooking. Dan's mother was an excellent cook of German descent and he had often shared memories of her meals.

By the time we finished our class, we had experimented with several recipes and purchased a German cookbook. Discovering that most German meals do not consist of large amounts of sausage and sauerkraut, we learned that fresh pork, ham, and bacon were popular meats in Germany. A traditional breakfast consisted of a large mug of hot coffee, freshly baked rolls, soft-cooked eggs, sausages, and an assortment of cheeses. Breakfast had already been a favorite meal at our house. On weekends when Eli was at home, we especially made a big deal of it trying new recipes such as a leek omelet, bacon pancakes, baked apples, cheese fritters and more until we could eat no more. Laughing, Eli decided that our next class should be an exercise class.

Eli called one evening when he was a senior in college to let us know he was bringing a friend home for the weekend and asked if that would be okay. The friend turned out to be Sarah, a lovely girl majoring in sociology. Eli literally had stars in his eyes. Talking to both Eli and God, Dan and I prayed that their relationship would evolve slowly and that they would become friends—first and foremost.

After going to bed that night, I searched my memory. Remembering Eli as the soft-spoken child who first showed up in my office so many years ago, I was awed at the amount of time that had passed and how we all had changed in very natural ways. God had surely blessed us. At the same time, I couldn't help but feel that something was missing in our lives. I fell asleep wondering.

The following Sunday my question was answered. Pastor Swenson, a wise, religious man with a booming voice, read the second reading from Hebrews, "….let us run with perseverance the race that is set before us, looking to Jesus the pioneer and perfecter of our faith, who for the sake of the joy that was set before him endured the cross…"

The sermon was about the responsibilities of discipleship. We ended the service singing, "Blest Be The Tie That Binds," the song from our wedding. Closing my bulletin, I noted the words at the bottom: "We leave to worship the Lord with our lives." I hadn't noticed them before. Being a Christian was not just about attending services on Sunday; it was also about what happened during the week. Knowing this, but needing a gentle reminder, I started to think differently about some things. Although it is impossible and we are so unworthy, we should strive to be as Christ-like as possible.

That week I joined a neighborhood Bible study made up of six to seven ladies from our community. We began our study with a booklet entitled, "Knowing God's Will." Dan joined a men's group who met at the same time. Sharing our thoughts when we both arrived home, it gave us an opportunity to grow in faith.

Meeting once a week, we became a close knit group, sharing our concerns after the Bible study lesson was completed and praying for each other. Because it was an introductory course, a couple of the ladies were new to the idea of a Bible study group. One did not know the order of the books of the Bible; another stumbled on certain words when she read; yet, when we prayed we all reached for each other's hands. A sense of being sisters of the faith permeated our gatherings although we were of different ages, professions, and family backgrounds.

Even though I felt at the time that my life was in order, I was reminded during our study that God had a plan for each of us. I found Proverbs 14:12, "What you think is the right road may lead to death," and Isaiah 55:8-9, "My thoughts, says the LORD, are not like yours, and my ways are different from yours," humbling. And, I began to re-think and spend more time praising and giving thanks for the abundant life that Christ had given me and understanding that God was not finished with me yet.

31

Sitting on a bluff overlooking the river, the house had a Spanish appeal. White stone bricks arched over a double garage and the main entrance to the house. It was sided with dark stain and roofed with shake shingles. The large entrance was floored with Spanish tile, and an elegant chandelier hung from a cathedral ceiling. A few steps led us to glass doors which opened to a cemented patio which overlooked trees, grasses, wildflowers, and the river below. Narrow wooden steps with a banister on one side connected the cemented patio to a dock where a small fishing boat was anchored.

The house had four bedrooms; three full bathrooms; a great room with kitchen, dining room, and family room together; a laundry room; and an office all nicely arranged on two floors. Signing a stack of paperwork, we settled with the realtor on our anniversary. Leaving the realtor's office that day, we hopped into Dan's car and started making mental lists of all the things we needed to do before moving. Looking for paper and a pen, I noticed cigarette ashes on the floor.

"Dan," I jokingly asked, "have you taken up smoking?"

"I smelled smoke, but I thought it was coming from outside the car," he answered.

"Someone's been in our car," I added becoming alarmed.

"Hmmm…someone made a mistake; got in the wrong car; that kind of thing," was Dan's attempt of reassurance.

"How could a person not know his own car?" I questioned.

"There are some odd people out there, Karen. Someone could have been confused; this is a pretty common model of car. Who knows." He dismissed it.

I looked around and saw nothing else that appeared to be suspicious. We went back to mental list making on our way home, but Dan's comment there are some odd people out there, Karen, caused me to think of Martin.

Moving was an adventure, one we never wanted to repeat. We had immediate possession of our new home while our old home was still on the market, so there was not a lot of pressure to get things done in a short period of time. However, with both of us working during the week, we tried to get a lot done on the weekends. With this pace, we discovered that we were often tired and grouchy all week long. Exhausted one Friday night, we fell into bed irritated with each other for no particular reason. Dan rolled over, took me into his arms, and asked me if I wanted to hear a joke.

"A joke? Are you kidding?" I asked. "It's midnight and I'm exhausted."

"Knock-knock." He said quietly running his finger tips up and down my ribs.

"You're asking me a knock-knock joke at midnight?" This was hilarious. I snuggled closer enjoying his warmth.

"Sure. Knock-knock." He persisted.

"Who's there?" I answered rolling my tired eyes.

"Banana."

"Banana?"

"You're supposed to say 'banana who?'"

"Banana, who?" I gave in.

"Knock-knock." He repeated.

"Who's there?" I was trying to be patient but I did have to smile .

"Banana."

"Banana, who?" I answered—getting it right.

"Knock-knock."

"Okay," I said. "Who's there?"

"Orange."

"Orange, who?" Now, it was getting interesting.

"Orange you glad I didn't say 'banana'?"

With that we both started laughing like kids considering the fact that we had both bought bananas on the way home from work to have for snacks while packing and unpacking and now had several pounds sitting on the kitchen counter waiting for someone, anyone to devour them.

The next day we hired a U-Haul, packed it and our car with kitchen items, including bananas, and headed to our river home. After moving in boxes, we locked the doors behind us and headed to the shoreline where we rented a pontoon boat. We spent several hours rejuvenating and floating the river. Later, we discovered an old diner where we ate grilled cheese on crusted whole wheat accompanied by large dill spears while scanning the walls covered with pictures of BIGGEST FISH CAUGHT. Dressed in billed caps, sweatshirts or plaid shirts, and jeans, the locals told their river stories. With frazzled whiskers, crooked smiles, and eyes the color of the sea, they enjoyed the bantering as much as we did. Feeling a sense of kinship and more relaxed than we had been in weeks, we returned to our river home to spend the night, thinking the kitchen items could be unpacked on a rainy day.

Months later, our house in town was empty and ready for new occupants; however, the river house was a different tale. We unpacked what we needed, but our list of things to do had as many fun activities as it did house projects. On the weekends, we attended the art and craft shows. We learned about the rarity of Mississippi pearls, and Dan later surprised me with a necklace on a romantic evening. The commute to our jobs each day was longer, but the trip was worth it. As the seasons changed, we were continually entertained by tens of thousands of birds migrating in the fall and returning in the spring, the white tailed deer, the bald eagles, changing leaves, wildflowers, a riverboat's blast after the spring ice vanished.

Eventually, we met the neighbors—lovers of the river all of them. Robert, our closest neighbor, invited Dan to go fishing one Saturday morning, and Dan was literally hooked for life. Eli visited a couple of weeks later, and the same happened to him. It was a good father-son pastime, and I never minded the time they spent together on the river. When Sarah tagged along, we hiked the trails, visited the many quaint shops in surrounding towns, and became friends.

During one July morning, the birthday club bunch ventured out to our river home for the first time. We celebrated a birthday with a German Sweet Chocolate cake and feasted on a variety of salads and breads the group had brought on the patio over-looking the river. Later, Dan piloted us on a pontoon boat ride. Stepping off the boat with slight cases of sunburn, they left around five p.m. chattering their thanks, and I responded with, "We'll do it again, soon."

After the last goodbyes, I headed to the deck to finish cleaning up. Any food scraps always attracted the wild creatures, and although we adored them from a distance, we did not appreciate them on the deck. Opening up the glass deck door, I looked down towards the river. As evening approached, the river turned into shades of purple as the trees reflected their various colors in the water. In other spots, the sunlight was blinding where it bounced off the water. With the various reflections affecting my vision, I sensed him before I saw him—a person sitting half way down to the river on our steps. Closing my eyes and then opening them to adjust to the darkness under the trees where the steps were located, I saw a man—a rather large man. With his back to me, his shoulders were hunched with his elbows placed on his knees. I entered the house leaving the deck door open.

"Dan," I called when in the house. Where was he?

"Dan," I tried again before locating him in the garage cleaning out his car. "Dan, there's a man sitting on our steps."

"What?" he questioned.

"A man. Sitting on our steps, on the way down to the dock."

Wiping his hands on his already dirty fishing shirt, he said nothing, took the garage steps in one leap and headed towards the deck doors. I had to run to keep up with him.

On the deck, we both looked below to see an empty staircase leading to the water.

"You're sure, Karen?" he asked.

"Yes. I'm sure. Do you have any idea who might…."

"I didn't want to say anything before," he interrupted, "but I've seen someone sitting on our steps before. A larger man, always with his back to the house. Whenever I've approached him, he's taken off."

"You're kidding me. Why didn't you tell me?"

"Well, I didn't want to scare you. You know, we've got a few hoboes around here, wanderers. Someone might have needed a shady spot to hang out."

"Well, it is a little strange, Dan. We're not exactly close to a town or a highway where he might get a handout or transportation."

Neither one of us knew what to say.

"Do you have any idea who it might be?" I asked. Looking down and with a hand on his chin, he slowly shook his head. Dan sat at the picnic table and I sat beside him.

We both looked down towards the river and then we scanned the trees and undergrowth as if they held an answer. Dan didn't have any idea who it might be, but I did. Although I had tried to ignore these happenings, the following thoughts tumbled through my head one after another like an old slide show: the bump in the back of the church on our wedding night, a tattered man walking the streets of our town with hunched shoulders, the stolen wedding pictures, a smoke filled car and, yes, there was more. Other things I had chosen not to pay attention to: a man standing by our mailbox looking towards our house, a frazzled but familiar looking person sitting in the stands at one or two of Eli's basketball games, a feeling of being followed in the grocery store, someone calling the school—asking for me—and then hanging up.

I took a deep breath, touched Dan's arm, and whispered, "I know who it is."

"Why are you whispering," he looked from side to side.

"I'm not sure. It's just kind of spooky."

"Why? Who?" he questioned.

"Why?" I questioned. "What…" Not following his thinking.

"Who, Karen? You said you thought you might know who it is."

"Martin."

"Martin? Martin, who?"

I had told Dan about Martin, my first marriage, the venereal disease. He knew I was on medication occasionally because of it and the precautions we needed to both take because of it. But Dan never held it against me, never brought it up as an issue. Talk about forgive and forget, Dan had done this to the point that the name Martin didn't even set off an alarm for him.

When I didn't answer his question, he repeated, "Martin who?"

With furrowed brow, I looked deep into his eyes, and he said, "Your first husband."

I nodded in affirmation, not wanting even to repeat Martin's name.

"Oh." Dan looked confused. I couldn't tell if he was trying to make light of this or feel threatened.

The following morning, after some discussion, we called the local sheriff to report our concerns. Thinking this would take care of it, we soon discovered that it did not. Everywhere we went, we were looking over our shoulders to see if someone was following us. When we got up in the morning, we checked the dock steps. Before we went to bed at night, we latched our windows and double latched our doors. We no longer felt comfortable letting the night breeze into our home on the main floor. Fear of what might happen was affecting our day to day routine and spontaneity. Was if safe for me to stay home alone? Was it safe for anyone to go down to the fishing dock alone? Should we lock the doors during the day, or just at night? When or if he comes again, should we confront him or just call the sheriff? Was he really dangerous, or was he just a lost soul who needed some help?

In my last conversation with Margo, when I asked about Martin, she stated that "no news was good news." Not wanting to worry her, I waited several weeks, and then I knew I must call. Dan and I decided that Martin's family had a right to know of his possible whereabouts.

Interestingly, Margo was somewhat relieved. She had personally worried that Martin had ended up in a big city, lived off the streets, gotten into drugs-- that kind of thing. When I asked for suggestions if he were to show up again, she hesitated before answering, "Just tell him to call home. We need to hear from him. Call collect. Just call."

"Of course, Margo." I could do that I reassured her.

"We really don't know how to love him, Karen. It's always been so hard. But we do love him. Please help him if you see him." I empathized with the yearning in her heart but soon felt an outpouring of sorrow. I had failed Martin; I had not loved him enough. I didn't know how to love him. I was moved to a simple prayer, "Dear God, forgive us. We are all so weak. We ask for your guidance in all things. To your glory."

I knew very little about mental illnesses, post traumatic stress syndrome, or any of that. However, I did know Martin had been unusual when we were married, and he certainly seemed to be more so, now. However, in the next few weeks, something completely took our minds off Martin. Something immense.

32

School was out! Students and staff were exuberant--another last day of school. Vacations, camps, swimming, picnics, and, in general, free-time topped the list of things to look forward to. Little did we know on that last day of school that the summer of 1993 would go down in history. Record amounts of rainfall soon started falling. Day after day, a shower here, a downpour there--it became more predictable than the sun shining. As we went about our daily tasks, those of us who lived alongside the river became uneasy. The river became more reckless than usual and was both fascinating and terrible to watch. Dan and I tried to continue with our usual routines, but the rain hammered down causing the river to take on a disordered personality.

By mid-July, the National Guard was sent out. By August 1, the river was declared unstable. We were fortunate that our home was located on a high bluff; however, some of our neighbors with homes closer to the waterfront had already taken what items they could, stored the rest, and fled. The Mighty Mississippi become erratic and fickle. Acting like an unruly child, Old Man River scattered wildlife and greedily gathered trees, plant life, and whatever debris he could glum on to with his bony crested fingers and took it downstream. We watched on the news as entire homes in some areas were devoured in seconds by the raging waters.

Dan and I felt helpless, then joined groups of volunteers who were helping with the flood effort. Some of us filled sandbags; others provided food. We did what we could—sometimes not knowing what day it was nor knowing when we had last slept. My parents showed up a couple of weekends to bring food and help with household chores so that Dan and I could continue our volunteer work. Eli and Sarah took off a week from work, brought old clothes, and worked filling sandbags. Our paradise turned into catastrophe. Exhausted, we listened to the nightly news. The

Army Corps of Engineers, the experts, and the locals all gave opinions from, "We're not giving up," to "It can't be stopped."

Hydrologists said such a flood was a 100-500 year event. Although it affected a nine state area and the losses were huge, Dan and I were fortunate. Our dock and steps leading to our river front could be rebuilt. Many, especially further down the river, had losses that could never be recuperated.

Our twentieth wedding anniversary arrived without us giving note. We were in the middle of a national disaster and remembering an anniversary was one of the last things on our minds. School started with every student having a story about the flood. So and so stayed with us; we filled sandbags; our basement flooded; we had to move out; etc. Although it was difficult for all of us to get into a school routine, by mid October, we felt that the students were finally settled.

Instead of celebrating our wedding anniversary in August, Dan and I set aside a day in late October to do so. Dan's plan was to take a week off from work and rebuild our dock and steps with the help of Robert, our neighbor. The river, like the students, had settled, but our surroundings would never be the same. We planned to celebrate the completion of the new dock and our anniversary with a quiet dinner at home—steaks on the grill, Texas toast, spinach salad, baked potatoes. October was a beautiful time of the year. Although many of our shore-line trees had been taken, we still had fall colors on those surrounding our house. Some of the previously scattered animals were slowly returning to their changed habitat. After the hectic summer, we were looking forward to a weekend alone.

Arriving home from school on Friday, I dropped my purse, lunch bag, and a Red Cross manual on the kitchen counter and headed for the deck to check out the progress of the steps and dock below. Delighted to see a completed stairway, sans banister, and completed dock, I rushed down the steps in hopes of spotting Dan. He was nowhere in sight. There were no tools left out, and I noticed that the fishing boat was gone. Placing my hand over my eyes for a sunshield, I scanned the river but saw nothing but muddy waters casually drifting their way to the sea.

Retracing my path, I returned to the house and phoned Robert.

"Hello." Robert answered on the second ring.

"Hi, Robert. Me, Karen. Is Dan with you?"

"Heck, no, Karen," he laughed. "You know Dan better than I do. Dock's finished. The man is fishing."

"What? We were going to…"

"Don't worry. He was just eager. We worked like dogs all day. Hasn't been out for a while, you know. With the dock done, he thought he'd try his luck before you came home. He'll be back."

"Sure. Thanks, Robert. And, also, thanks for helping with the dock. I can't believe you guys are done already."

"Sure," Robert laughed. "You guys owe us. Mary and I would come over and help you with those steaks but the kids have a band concert tonight. We'll catch you later." And with that, he hung up.

River men in Mark Twain's day knew that certain stretches of the Mississippi River were treacherous. Sunken rocks and submerged islands refused to stay put in the hurried river currents. These narrow channels became known as graveyards. Later, the Corps of Engineers removed these rocks and the islands somehow attached themselves to various banks. However, the river had just recently torn up and swallowed whatever was in its path while rushing to the sea invading both rural and urban areas. It had been declared unstable. Why had Dan gone fishing? The river he had loved to fish in last spring was not the same river today.

I waited to start supper. Six o'clock arrived and then seven o'clock. I called Robert. No answer. I had forgotten he and his wife were at a school event. Every fifteen minutes, I took the new, unpainted steps down to the dock and looked up and down the river. Nothing. Mosquitoes annoyed me. For October, it was hot and humid. I felt sweaty and sick to my stomach and thought about taking a shower but did not want to be away from the phone or away from the dock too long.

When darkness arrived, I knew Dan was in trouble. He would not stay out after dark. He never had. I called the sheriff and reported him missing and gave as many details as I could. Next, I called Eli. Feeling the heaviness in his heart over the news, it pained me greatly to tell him. Finally, I called my parents who were almost out the door before my phone call ended. Leaving the house to take another trip down to the dock, I saw car lights in Robert's driveway and took the path between our homes.

As he and his wife and two children were entering the house, I approached Robert.

"Robert." I was having difficulty speaking. "I need to talk to you."

He knew by looking at me that something was terribly wrong.

"What is it?" He would not take his eyes off me as he told his children to go with their mother into the house and get ready for bed.

"It's Dan. He's not home."

"You're sure?"

"Yes, he's not home."

"We need to call…"

"I've already called the county sheriff. I don't know what else to do."

Robert touched my arm briefly. "Dan's a smart man. He's probably stranded somewhere, and it's taking him a while to get back."

"I'm sick with worry. What should we do? What can we do?" I pleaded.

"Let's take another look," Robert suggested, and we headed for the dock.

My legs feeling lifeless, I followed Robert down the steps, and we approached the end of the dock reluctantly. The water softly lapped the support posts below. Stars overhead hinted of something more, and a soft breeze gave me a bit of hope. My emotional state took a nose-dive, however, when I viewed the murky dark water. Sickened, I dropped to my knees and started retching.

Robert stood by, helpless. There was nothing to say. He knelt beside me and rubbed my back. When I was done, he took my hand and we returned to the house. Robert turned on some lights and called his wife. While he was speaking on the phone, car lights lit our drive. Robert gravely greeted my parents at the door, quietly shared a few words, and then left. A few moments later, Eli and Sarah arrived and let themselves in. I hugged them both as we exchanged worried looks.

"No news?" Eli asked.

"No news," I replied.

Eli left the house. I knew he was headed for the dock. I didn't have the heart to tell him that he would see nothing but darkness. A few moments later, more car lights reflected off the windows and escaped into our home. There was a knock on the door. My parents rose to answer it and motioned for me to sit. Sarah took my hand and knelt beside me wondering at the same time when Eli would return. The Sheriff and my parents shared a few words and then he approached my chair. I was prepared to hear the worst.

"Karen, may I call you Karen?" He looked deep into my eyes. He had done this before—delivered the worst of news.

"Karen, your husband's fishing boat was discovered in the middle of the river circling on its own. Some fishermen were able to stop it. They retrieved your husband's billfold. We're not sure of Dan's whereabouts right now, but it looks like some kind of accident may have happened."

"Accident? What do you mean? The boat's okay, right? Where is he?" I questioned.

"He was not in the boat. He may have fallen out. He may have…. Karen, did Dan have any heart condition or other medical issues?"

"No. Nothing. I don't understand."

"We don't either. But, we will continue to look for him." And, with that he rose somewhat awkwardly and turned to leave as Eli entered the house. He and Eli spoke several minutes and then the headlights swept through our house again and were gone.

I turned to my dad who had been silent so far.

"What can we do?" I asked my dad knowing he had no answer.

"Karen, we all have been praying ever since we heard that Dan was missing." He choked on his words as he spoke. "We need to continue praying knowing that Dan is in God's care where ever he is."

And, with that, we all joined hands—each of us pleading for God's mercy and grace, asking that Dan be safe, asking for hope. The grandfather clock in the corner of the great room ticked its minutes confidently. The refrigerator hummed softy in the kitchen. Shadows danced across the sparsely-lit family room as the wind nudged the tree limbs back and forth outside allowing the moon's rays a peek at our small family circle. Eli and Sarah fell asleep in each other's arms on the floor. Covering them with a comforter, I noticed their tear-stained faces. My mother slept quietly, her head resting on Dad's shoulder. My dad stared at the trees outside, his lips in unceasing prayer.

Sitting by the phone, exhausted and achy from worry, I let my mind wander. Seeing Dan in church with Eli for the first time, Dan showing up at the singles' picnic feeling a bit awkward, Dan calling about Eli's swimmer's ear, Dan in my office stating his intentions to get to know me better, our first date, the wedding, the conversation in the church about the ring he had chosen for me, the boat house honeymoon, moving and our new home. I could not stand the waiting.

I jumped as the clock chimed 4 a.m. Dad snored quietly, his lips still mumbling as he slept. Quietly, I showered, letting the water go both very hot and very cold hoping to feel something besides terrible dread. Wiping the condensation from a clouded mirror, I saw an unfamiliar person. Worry had taken its toll: matted hair, swollen eyes, pale faced. I pulled on an old pair of jeans and a tee shirt, left the house, and once again took the dock steps down to the river below. Although it was still dark, a heavy fog was evident. The steps were dewy and a fine mist hung in the air. I tried to view the river, but I could barely see my hand in front of my face. Once again, my eyes looked down at the waves quietly slapping the dock posts—murky waters with a secret. The river knew.

Returning up the steps, I passed the house, ventured down the driveway and out onto the road. Needing to clear my head, I started walking with no destination in mind. The fog exaggerated the early morning sounds; everything felt close but not within reach. A back door opened; a garbage can was set out. Someone talked on another back porch. A car started. I heard the crunch of gravel underfoot, and the tweet-tweet of a bird just above me but unseen. Thinking the bird's song a good omen, I searched for it. "Tweet-tweet," I quietly murmured. "Tweet-tweet," it returned. And, then I saw it—a red-winged blackbird dipping its wings and singing barely two feet from my right shoulder. I gazed at it, wanting to believe it was a good sign. Then, with a final dip of its wing and a last "tweet," blackbird disappeared into the early morning thickness. Dan was gone; I knew it. The river had taken him.

For I am the Lord your God who churns up the sea so that its waves roar, the Lord Almighty is his name. I have put my words in your mouth and covered you with the shadow of your hand—I who set the heavens in place, who laid the foundations of the earth, and who say to Zion, "You are my people." Isaiah 51.

Having been washed ashore, Dan's body was found downstream several days later. An autopsy report indicated a massive heart attack. The funeral was several days later. Pastor Swenson did his best, saying all the right things that could be said. The church was full—a mix of black and blue colors, some with tears, all solemn. Besides my own grief, my concern for Eli was enormous. As a child, he had lost his mother and grandmother to cancer and now this. How would he handle it? He had been so close to his father. I was thankful he had Sarah in his life. Dan had shared his faith in God with Eli, and I knew that, with time, Eli would survive.

Eli did most of the funeral planning. Some of his dad's favorite songs— *In the morning when I rise give me Jesus…you may have all the rest, give me Jesus… and Morning is broken like the first morning…* I couldn't sing them. I had no voice; the lump in my throat was too large. Dan had loved the morning and life in general. I would be lost without him.

33

I decided not to return to school until the second semester. After the funeral, Eli and Sarah stayed for a week—reminiscing. Eli would sort through his father's things later—much later, if need be. After that first week, I tried being alone. It didn't work. I had no interest in using the dock that Dan had built. I did not want to even look at the river. The house was big and hollow without him. I could not sleep nor did I have much interest in eating. The house didn't need to be cleaned or picked up; there were no dirty clothes; the cupboards were full with no one to eat with. There were no shops to visit or hikes to be taken. One views the world differently when all of a sudden one is alone.

After a couple of sleepless nights listening to every hum and creak from the house, I crawled out of bed one morning, packed a few items, locked the house, got into our car, and took off for my parents' place. They had moved off the farm and into town several years before, so the outside of the house was different. But, inside, was a different story—same furniture, same pictures on the walls, same items in the cupboards, same rugs on the floor. As long as Mom and Dad lived within, I could call it home. Not surprised to see me, they welcomed me with open arms and led me to the extra bedroom to put my things. Not really being into decorating, Mom had used the same bedspread and curtains I had in my room during my high school years. The furniture was even placed as it was years ago. It was like going back in a time machine every time I visited.

"Karen," she called from the kitchen, "when you're settled, come out to the table. Dad and I have something to show you."

Leaving my few packed items on the bed, I kicked off my shoes and padded down the hallway to the kitchen.

"Hi, Honey." She looked at Dad. "We're glad you came."

"Thanks Mom. I should have called. I just didn't. Nothing's the same."

"We can not begin to imagine what it must be like for you," Mom sympathized. "You can stay as long as you like."

"Thank you….did you have something to show me?"

"Well, we have gotten lots of sympathy cards from old friends and neighbors. They probably didn't know your address. Anyway, when you feel like it, you can read them."

"Sure…."

"Also, Dad and I were going through some old boxes we brought in from the farm. I guess we had forgotten about them—being busy farming, raising you kids, but there are some real interesting photographs. Maybe tomorrow, we'll take a look," she suggested.

"Mom, it's only mid-morning; let's take a look," I tried smiling. They were being so careful.

Dad brought out a large black worn metal box and placed it by Mom's chair. Mom carefully opened the top as if treasure were inside and placed an item wrapped in yellowed tissue on her lap. She carefully unfolded the tissue to reveal a large black and white photo of a beautiful woman. I guessed her to be about thirty years of age. With high cheekbones, dark eyes, and black hair, I noted the family resemblance.

Mom took a deep breath and announced, "This is Fannie, your great grandmother. You remember the story?"

"She's beautiful. She was Indian, I know. We always knew the story— falling in love with Great Grandpa on the way to the Gold Rush and eventually returning to her tribe and the river after he left her. But, I didn't know you had pictures."

"I guess we just forgot, or like I said, we were just too busy to remember. These pictures mean more to us now than they would have years ago."

"There's more?" I questioned trying to peek into the box.

"Oh, yes," and with that, she pulled out more photos wrapped in yellowed tissue paper along with a tattered obituary from a newspaper regarding Great Grandpa's death. Thus we spent our first day—wondering what life was like for Great Grandpa and Fannie so long ago.

I spent a week with my parents. We breakfasted, lunched and supped together. There was always a prayer before meals and after. Dad would often share his favorite Bible verses after the evening meal. One of his favorites, Romans 8: 38-39, became one of mine.

"For I am sure that neither death, nor life, nor angels, nor principalities, nor things present, nor things to come, nor powers, nor height, nor death, nor anything else in all creation, will be able to separate us from the love of God in Christ Jesus our Lord."

Dad, my father and my friend, was everything a dad should be. His faith constantly inspired me and revived my weary spirit. "Pray for peace and understanding, Karen. God truly loves and cares for you."

With a journal full of Bible verses and the large picture of Fannie, I returned to my home on the river. November arrived. Following a routine helped fill my time. I planned a Thanksgiving meal, started a Christmas list, and joined a grief support group. The birthday club came for their November celebration—somewhat hesitantly—but they did come. After a few tears and how are you doing, we miss you at work, we mindlessly played a few hands of cards and enjoyed a meal. It wasn't the same, but it was and that was a start.

Returning to normal shopping and errand-running, I sensed that some people treated me differently. A few acquaintances avoided contact either by taking another aisle in the grocery store or crossing the street so they wouldn't have to speak. Others more or less pretended not to know me or remember who I was. People didn't know how to deal with death. Others who were comfortable with talking to me asked, "How are you doing, Karen?" I would always say, "Fine." Someone else asked, "How do you do it?" I smiled and said, "You just do," but admitted to myself that most of the time I didn't.

Some gave advice freely and talked non-stop seeming not to know when to stop. *Do you need a hug?* No thank you. I don't want to be touched. *I think you should…* I'm sorry, I'm not listening any more. *Take care of yourself. You need to eat.* The fresh fruit you brought decayed on the kitchen counter. *Invite new people into your life.* I'm sorry, but I can barely remember you; why would I want to meet someone new? *It's okay to ask for help.* No thank you; I don't need any. Please go away.

One very gray day, I couldn't force myself out of bed. With despair as my only companion, I looked around the room. A tweed overcoat, size 10, hung in the corner and reminded me of the fact that Dan was once a boy. When we moved into our river house, I discovered the coat while rummaging through his boyhood boxes. I had placed it on a special antique hook on a wall of our bedroom because I enjoyed imagining him during this time of his life. What was he like? Would he have liked me? Karen and Dan sitting in a tree. K-i.-s-s-i-n-g. First comes loves. Then, comes marriage. Then comes Karen with the…. No baby. If I had known

Dan in elementary school or even high school or before Martin, maybe there would have been a baby. Our baby.

On the wall opposite the bed, three family pictures were neatly arranged along with a dried floral arrangement—now dust covered. One was a picture of Dan as an infant, eyelashes fanning soft, pink cheeks. Another picture had two poses of Dan around four or five, dressed in shorts and matching jacket. Dan was holding a book, but the twinkle in his eye was focused on the camera. In the third picture, he sat with legs crossed looking off into the distance.

My attention was drawn to the stately bedposts. Dan and I had chosen this walnut bed because of the elaborate head and footboards and sturdy posts anchoring each corner. A worn plaid robe of Dan's hung on his side. He had loved it: faded, soft, brown. I knew his slippers were still under the bed beneath his robe. On my side hung a white cotton nightgown, almost limp to the touch. I had not worn it since his death preferring an old tee shirt.

A clock's tick-tock broke the silence and reminded me that I really needed to get up and do something—anything. But, you see, none of this stuff and none of what I thought I might need to do really meant anything any more. With Dan gone, it had no meaning, no significance, no pull. These things, his things, my things, used to bring me a certain amount of pleasure. The pictures, the bed we shared, his soft robe, all seemed senseless.

Rolling over on my side, I brought up my knees with an effort and dropped my feet to the floor. Noting the prayer book beside the bed, <u>Too Busy to Pray</u>, I thought of the irony. Too busy. I randomly turned to page forty and read.

It is dismal and gray outside, Lord.
It is dismal and gray inside, too.
I have a dreary mind today.
All I can drag from it are dull, lifeless thoughts and sterile prayers.
No good comes from a dreary mind Lord.

As I looked outside my window, my surroundings appeared to be bleak, cold, isolated. And, yet, inside a hint of hope was growing. I had read somewhere that every action has a ripple effect intended or not, and I thought of the seedlings buried deep beneath the blanket of snow even now beginning to wiggle and squirm and seek the sun. The scene outside would change as would my heart inside, day by day, week by week, by God's grace.

Returning to the book, checking out the front of the book, I read that Jo Carr and Imogene Sorley, authors, start with, "It's just me, Lord, talking to you about things as they are." A handwritten note by my mother read, "To Karen. Never be too busy to pray." Simply realizing that others were grieving as I was helped. Getting down on my knees, I took a deep breath and prayed, "Forgive me Lord. I need your help."

One rainy evening, I settled onto the couch with a blanket and the sympathy cards that had been sent. My parents and Eli and Sarah had helped with thank yous for memorials, but I had spent little time reading the cards. Wanting to go through them again, I decided to read a few each evening. So many had such good and kind things to say about Dan. He had been truly loved and respected by many.

Dan's work partner wrote, "Dan often spoke of you and Eli. Family was very important to him. He also had a deep faith in God. You will be in our thoughts and prayers, Karen." He closed with a verse from Deuteronomy. 33:27—"The eternal God is your dwelling place and underneath are the everlasting arms."

Another card stated simply, "Mrs. Wilson, Please know I care. You were so important during my growing up years. I'm so sorry for your loss." Signed, "Liddie."

Liddie Meyers-Jenkins. She had graduated, I knew, and had planned to go to nursing school. I looked at the post-mark. It was from a town several miles away.

Grabbing a local newspaper several weeks later and buying a hot cup of coffee, I thumbed through the paper at a café near my house. Skipping over the school sports, school lunch menus, up-coming holiday concerts, I flipped to the social page where I saw several engagement pictures and one wedding announcement. The caption read Meyers-Jenkins weds Hasbrow. Liddie? Could it be? I read further. …. Liddie Meyers-Jenkins, daughter of…. Married in St. Thomas Islands… graduate of nursing school….employed by… Mark Hasbrow, according to the paper, was the son of a local real estate agent and a graduate of the state business school. Liddie had done well. Making a mental note to call her, I left with a less-heavy heart.

Eli and Sarah visited often. I didn't know if they were doing it for me or if Eli needed to be in his father's home. One weekend, he suggested fishing.

"Let's go, Mom." With both elbows on the kitchen counter he stared at me. He had his dad's eyes. I couldn't say no.

"Well, you know, Eli, I'm not sure where all the gear is. I haven't really paid attention to that area of the garage since Dan…." I stopped and looked out the window down to the river. Robert had finished the banister and treated the dock and steps with a stain. I had seen him, occasionally, treading the steps downward to check the boat and dock—especially when inclement weather was predicted.

"It's ready to go, Mom." He was still looking at me. "I've got everything down on the dock. It's too cold to be out in the boat, but we'll try it from the dock—for old time's sake."

" What about Sarah? Does she want to come?"

"No. We've talked. She's in charge of lunch." Turning to her, he reassured himself, "Aren't you honey?"

"You bet. And, I've got some reading to do, too, for a class I'm taking. You and Eli go ahead. Lunch will be ready when you come back."

Eli and I bundled up in warm coats and light work gloves. It was November—not a good fishing month. We baited our hooks, threw a line out in the morning sunshine, and watched it plunk into the water and drift with the current. I had been avoiding the dock that Dan had built feeling that the task itself was responsible for Dan's death—the cause of his heart attack. And, of course, the river played a big part. If he hadn't been so drawn to it, if he hadn't felt the urge to go fishing, if, if, if…. Lately, if it wasn't if, it was why… I knew that none of these questions could be answered. It didn't stop me from asking them.

"Mom," Eli interrupted my thoughts. "Are you warm enough?"

"Sure. It feels good. To be here. I didn't think it would. But, it's okay."

"I'm glad, because Dad really loved it. He loved this place—the house, the river, the fishing, the animals. It's only right that you should continue to enjoy it. It will be different, but it's going to be okay, Mom."

Wondering how this son of Dan's and this man who called me Mom, could be so wise, a warm feeling washed over me.

"I've been thinking about this a lot," Eli continued. "In General Science, many years ago," he chuckled at this, "we learned that a river gathers strength as it flows. Sarah and I have been studying the Bible lately, and I found a verse that fits with that idea. It's in James. I can't recite it from memory yet, but I'd like to share it with you when we go back to the house."

"That's a fine idea, Eli." Almost breaking into tears, I continued, "Your dad was so proud of you."

We sat for another half hour or so watching the river flow past, listening to the birds overhead heading south, and breathing cool November air. Sarah called out "time for lunch" from the house, and we realized how hungry we were. It was a good feeling. She had prepared a simple lunch of chicken noodle soup and garlic bread. As Sarah started a pot of freshly brewed coffee and placed a pan of chocolate chip cookies in the oven, Eli brought the family Bible to the kitchen table and started reading the verse from James.

"This is it, Mom. It's from James, Chapter 1, starting with verse two… 'My brothers consider yourselves fortunate when all kinds of trials come your way. For you know that when your faith succeeds in facing such trials, the result is the ability to endure. Make sure that your endurance carries you all the way without failing so that you may be perfect and complete lacking nothing.'" He paused, "What do you think?"

"It's hard, Eli, to be thankful for trials, especially this one. But, I do know that without God, I would find this an impossible situation. Does that mean that I'm at least headed in the right direction?"

34

Thanksgiving was quiet. We had it at the river—Mom and Dad, both of my brothers and their families, and Eli and Sarah were all there. With a stuffed turkey in the oven, I set the table with our best dishes, placemats, and silverware. Mom arrived with pies—pumpkin and apple—homemade of course. Eli and Sarah, being on a vegetarian kick, brought a baked cheesy carrot dish and creamed onions. Josh's family brought relishes, and Zeke and his wife brought whole wheat rolls and corn bread. While some of us peeled potatoes, others were in and out of the house, checking the dock, enjoying the river. Josh and Zeke helped Eli sort some of Dan's stuff in the garage. I was so glad to have them all there and yet a great emptiness existed. Someone was missing and would never return. How would I ever get over that?

The dinner conversation was subdued. Work, politics, sports, when-Dan-was-here, etc. I was glad they were talking about him. Dan could not be forgotten. As we finished with pie and coffee, snow started to drift through the trees. Noticing it, the first of the season, we all moved to the large windows facing the river. Huge flakes, the size of half dollars, softly fell. Some of them found rest in the trees; others blanketed the various colors of fallen leaves on the ground. The flakes falling over the river disappeared as quickly as they landed, the river melting them like cotton candy melts in your mouth before you can even swallow it.

Everyone stayed overnight. Falling asleep with a full house, I slept a sleep I had not slept since Dan's death. It was good to be with family. In the morning, we pulled out the leftovers and had a Thanksgiving left-over breakfast. At around 10 a.m., with the sun melting off the white carpet accumulated the night before, everyone headed for home.

"Karen, are you going to be all right?" my mom asked.

"Mom, this has been a wonderful couple of days for me. But, I know you can't all stay. I'll be going back to work soon, so I'll keep busy. Please, don't worry."

"We'll keep in touch. Call whenever you want. Remember, it's Christmas at our house."

The following week, I decorated the house simply. There would be no outdoor lights or large tree this year. With a small tree in the great room and a nativity scene over the fireplace, it would have to do. On one wall of the family room, I placed Fannie's picture with other family portraits. Liddie's phone number was listed on my Christmas shopping list, and I decided to give her a call before I headed out. Just maybe she would be able to have lunch with me.

We met at a small Italian restaurant located along the river. Liddie drove up with a huge smile on her face. She had become a lovely young woman—a new bride with a college education and a job as one of the head nurses at the Good Samaritan Rehab Center. We celebrated our get-together by ordering somewhat exotically—escargot cavatore and pomodore con mozzarella for an appetizer. After some conversation about what college was like for her compared to my education, we ordered pasta and steamed asparagus. As we waited for our order, the conversation turned to a serious note.

"Mrs. Wilson…," Liddie started.

"Liddie, please call me Karen."

She smiled briefly before continuing, "Karen, please, tell me about Dan. I never really knew him. You were married a lot of years."

"It was an accident—a heart attack—while fishing. He had just finished replacing our dock and steps that day and decided to go fishing. He really loved the water, the animals, our home, the river. I don't know why it had to happen. I guess it's not for me to know why."

Liddie looked down. I remembered hearing about her sexual abuse as a child and felt sorry that I had even tried to gain her sympathy. We all had issues.

"I don't know what to say. I can't imagine what it must be like. Mark and I just got married and already I can't imagine life without him."

Smiling at her, I briefly touched her hand. "It's been a fairly short time since Dan's death. Some days I do okay; some days, I can't leave the house. I'm returning to work soon, and I think it will help me to stay busy—you know, be focused on others."

She thought for a while, took a bite or two of her pasta, and then put her fork down emphatically. "I hope I'm not being pushy, but I do have an idea. We really need volunteers at the Rehab. If you like, if you're not too busy when you go back to work, we could really use someone like you."

"…to do what?" Liddie had at least made me curious.

"Well, some come in to read to the clients; others write letters for them; some volunteers help out during field or road trips; and, of course, we always have the volunteers who come in on activity day to help with crafts and that kind of thing."

Remembering what was written on the bottom of our church bulletin—"We leave to worship the Lord with our lives," I caught myself nodding a yes to Liddie.

"Yes, I would like to know more. Is there a training session? Do I need to speak to someone?"

"I'll give Ruby, our administrator, your name. I'm sure there will be a background check, and, then, someone will get a hold of you, visit with you, that kind of thing, about what type of volunteer activities you would be interested in."

"Great. I can't promise you, Liddie, that anything will come of this, but I would like to check into it, and I appreciate your mentioning it. It has been so good to have this time with you…." Liddie interrupted me, "It has been good. You know, Mrs. Wilson, Karen, I don't believe I ever told you about the impact you had on my life. You saw a side of me that many others didn't. Before I met you, I felt like the girl from the other side of the tracks, the 'poor me' girl without a chance to do anything with her life. I need to thank you for that. I looked up to you. You believed in me. You saw me as a person of worth…."

She had tears in her eyes. Not knowing what to say to her, I handed her a tissue from my purse.

"This was a great idea—even if it was mine," I teased. "Let's do it again."

35

Christmas arrived. The best part was the Christmas Eve service and the children's program held at my parents' church. A live nativity scene held everyone's attention outside the church as the snow fell softy. With Mary and Joseph, the shepherds, the Wise Men, and a doll wrapped in swaddling clothes lying in the manger, everyone studied the scene quietly. The animals studied us in return. The wonder of Christmas blanketed us like a spell. Imagining what it would be like with Dan there, a huge lump formed in my throat. Knowing it would come out as a mournful cry, I took a deep breath and concentrated on the scene before me. Christ came that we might live eternally. To be absent in the body is to be present in the Lord. Where had I heard that? Was it from the Bible? Dan was with his Savior. What more could I want for him? He was in a glorious place, a place where, one day, we would be together again. Praise be to God.

My grief had caused me to shrink, to live small. This was all so against God's plan to make apparent His glory within us. I knew I must go forward. Only with God's grace could I do this.

I returned to work and my job as the school nurse after Christmas vacation. I was not prepared in any way. Thinking that everything would be the same, I discovered nothing was. After sleeping fitfully, I rose earlier than normal. It was a good thing as nothing fit me; my clothes hung limply. During the past couple of months I had spent very little time in front of a mirror. Now, on this morning, I looked like a bag lady. My clothes hung loosely, my hair was stringy and longer than usual, dark circles gave me a haunted appearance. Not wanting to elicit others' sympathy, wanting to return to work and fit in as before, I was in a panic. Pulling my hair back in a ponytail, I dressed in layers, applied a little extra makeup under the eyes and a little extra rouge on the cheekbones.

Locking the house, I realized I had not packed lunch and the gas tank gauge was on low. Could I do this? When was the right time to go back? As

I walked into the office, Cheryl gave a quick hug and mentioned that there were notes on my desk. Any questions—just ask. Walking into my office, I felt as if it were my first day on the job. Although it all looked familiar, I didn't know where to start. What should I do first? Hanging up my heavy winter coat and sticking my purse under my desk, I started to look at the notes when students started arriving for morning meds.

"Ms. Wilson, you're back!" One of them smiled. I knew him, but what was his name, and where was the key to the student medication drawer? Walking to the outer office, I tapped Cheryl on the shoulder.

"I need some help, Cheryl; this is more than I thought it would be. If you could just spend a few minutes with me until I get started."

Without a second look, Cheryl issued another hug, and we both headed back to the nurse's office. She stayed with me until morning meds were given and I had gone through the stack of notes.

"There's tomato soup with grilled cheese today. I'll bring your lunch in to you; we'll eat together. 11:30. Will that work for you?" She asked. What a blessing she was.

"How did you know I had forgotten my lunch?" I asked.

"I didn't. I just know you like tomato soup and grilled cheese." She smiled. I needed that.

The winter was cold, wet, and dreary; however, each day passed quickly and things fell into place. I grew used to the night sounds but felt I would never grow used to sleeping alone. On the weekends I started volunteering at the Good Samaritan Rehab where Liddie worked. Writing letters, reading newspapers and playing cards with some of the residents was rewarding. Most of them were quiet; I didn't need to say a lot. I just needed to be there. Most of the residents were elderly; however, there were a few men who were Vietnam War veterans with various injuries which made living in a rehab center helpful. I felt sorry for them. Being relatively young, they apparently didn't have families who could give the kind of care they needed.

One Saturday in February, Ruby met me as I was taking off my coat.

"Karen, we need a card player today. How are you at rummy?"

"Rummy? Which one?" I kidded. There were many versions.

"Oh, don't worry. They'll let you know the rules. There's an open spot at one of the tables. Have a seat. I'll bring you a diet soda."

Approaching the empty spot, I recognized Lilly, a lively 85 year old, and Wilbur, in his motorized wheelchair sitting across from each other.

Lilly was already shuffling the cards. Sitting down, I greeted both of them and started to introduce myself to my partner. Sticking my hand across the table, I started to speak and then stopped and pulled my hand back. He said nothing; he only stared at me as I was at him. Neither of us could believe what we saw.

"Hi, I'm Karen." I had to say something even though I knew this man.

"I know...." Martin said. "You're Karen."

I wanted to ask a thousand questions. What are you doing here? Why didn't I know you were here? Why didn't I notice you before? How long have you been here? But, I could ask none. Lilly dealt the cards. My hands shook. I placed them on my lap to hide them, but my breathing was irregular. When he stopped staring to focus on his own cards, I studied him. Unkempt but clean, wrinkled and worn looking, he had aged considerably. I pretended not to know him. We discussed our rummy hands, the weather. Lilly and Wilbur smiled at each other—romance apparently still alive at their age. After several games, it was snack time and Wilbur motored off with Lilly following in her walker. Martin and I were alone.

"Karen." His voice was hoarse and aged. "I'm sorry for your loss. Your husband. He died, didn't he?"

"Yes. He did." Wanting to get up and leave, I could not. I needed to know more.

"Martin, what are you doing here?"

He rubbed his slightly bearded face. "Post traumatic syndrome. Stuff like that. Ask my doc. He'll tell you."

"I'm sorry." I didn't know what else to say.

"It's not bad. Being here. Food's good. Company could be better. There's more like me. Jim. Butch. We talk. Sometimes."

My chair screeched loudly as I slid it back from the card table. Martin remained seated staring at me off and on.

"I guess it's snack time." With that I started to leave. All of the nice to see you, hope to see you again phrases couldn't be used. He rose, his chair screeching. I noticed the weight gain and his slumped shoulders—once so square and strong.

"Karen. I'm sorry. For your loss. Your husband. He died didn't he? Was it the river?"

Turning on shaky legs, I walked to the nearest door and exited.

36

Parking at McDonald's, I looked around but did not see Liddie's car. While waiting for her, I pushed the seat back into recliner position, turned off the car, and turned my face to the sun. If I could forget everything for a while, if I could clear my mind, maybe the unremitting headache in my skull would find another location. I often awoke in the middle of the night thinking, thinking, thinking—it never stopped. I missed Dan terribly. One day while traveling on the highway, I thought of how easy it would be to pull in front of a semi. It would be over. An accident. She fell asleep at the wheel, they would say. The semi driver would go uninjured. Knowing I could never carry it out, it was just a thought—a bad one. And Martin. What was Martin doing in the Rehab Center? Did his family know his whereabouts? Was he considered safe? Surely Liddie could give me some answers.

After ordering cheeseburgers, fries, and a diet soda, I started to question Liddie immediately.

"Why do you need to know?" Puzzled, she had picked up on my anxiety.

"I used to be married to Martin."

"You what?"

"I used to be married to Martin Christiansen. I used to be Mrs. Martin Christiansen. I know it sounds strange. It was many, many years ago."

"Oh, my gosh. Wow." She studied me. "What a small world, right?"

"You could look at it that way. Or, you could look at it… I don't want to jump to any conclusions, and I know I can't ask you to share confidential information—it's just a little alarming to me. How could he end up in the same area as I did?"

"Well, I can assure you, Karen, that Martin needs the kind of care that Good Samaritan provides. How he got here, I don't know."

"What's wrong with him?"

"I know there are some post-traumatic syndrome issues. Plus Martin is a complicated basket of mixed concerns." She hesitated. "He's probably one of the most complicated clients we have. I've seen mention of everything from separation anxiety as a child to anti-social behaviors to personality disorders in his file."

"How long has he been living at the center?" I questioned.

"Not long at all. I think he came about the same time I did."

"Is he considered 'safe'?"

"I'm not sure what you mean?"

"Will he hurt anyone?"

"We've never seen that part of him, Karen. He seems to be confused a lot. I've never considered him to be a threat to anyone."

That evening, I dug out Margo's phone number. It had been years since we'd spoken. I had received a sympathy card from her but she had been unable to come to Dan's funeral.

"Hello?" a young voice answered the phone after several rings.

"Uhhh…is your mother there?" I tried.

"Mom…." She yelled. Hearing a clunk on the other end, I figured that she had run off to get her mother.

After much background noise, Margo answered, out of breath. "Hello."

"Hi, Margo? It's Karen. Karen Wilson."

"Karen. Wow. How are you? I'm so sorry. I couldn't come. How are you doing?" It all rushed out.

"Yes, I'm doing okay. Thank you for the card. How have you been?"

"Well, as you can probably tell with all this noise, we have a full house. Never a dull moment."

"Please tell me about your family…" and she did so having to stop every so often to quiet a child or answer a question.

"But, Karen, we need to talk about you. Again, I'm so sorry I didn't make it. Is there anything I can do?"

"It's not easy, of course. Dan was pretty special. And, of course, Eli…" I had to stop. I couldn't really talk about it with all the background noise at Margo's house. Needing quiet and feeling guilty for needing it when Margo had none—or any promise of it soon—I just wanted my questions answered.

"Margo, I need to ask you about Martin. He lives in a rehab center here in town. Did you know that?"

"Yes, of course, I did. I couldn't tell you Karen. Martin moved in at about the same time as Dan's funeral. The timing was all wrong. I just hoped you would never run into him."

"Why?" I questioned.

"Uhhhh… Why? Why did I not tell you? Why was the timing wrong?"

"What's wrong with Martin? Why is he there?"

"Oh. Martin had some post traumatic syndrome issues. Plus, you're aware of everything else he was carrying around. You probably understood just as well as any of the rest of his family."

"I'm not sure I ever did."

"I've visited him just once. The kids keep me pretty tied down. But, he does seem to be adjusted. He also has a few buddies there—guys with somewhat similar circumstances."

"I was just surprised to see him—to say the least."

"How did you run into him?"

"I volunteer at the rehab center."

"Oh my gosh. I am sorry, Karen; I really should have told you."

"I understand. I'd better let you go. You sound really busy."

"Karen, remember what I told you a long time ago? If you see Martin—just tell him his family loves him. Mom and Dad can't really get there anymore, and I'm often tied down. He really doesn't have much. I know it's asking a lot, but I think he needs to hear it. We all do. He's not an exception." She hesitated. "I'm so sorry to ask it of you; the timing is really wrong….."

"Margo, he's your brother. It's obvious you love and care for him in spite of everything that has happened. I'll do what I can."

"Love you, Karen. Take care."

"Love you, Margo."

I read somewhere that everyone has four faces: one the world knows, one our friends know, one we know ourselves, and one God knows. The world didn't know Martin; he had sequestered himself. Did he even have friends? He didn't seem capable of realistic introspection. However, God did know him.

Dr. Henrietta C. Mears in her book <u>What the Bible is All About</u> wrote, "When you are in the will of God, things do not just happen. No friend crosses your path by accident. No joy or sorrow comes into your life except by God's permission."

37

Winter became spring. Seasons passed. Someone said, "Time waits for no one." Eli and Sarah had a child. Being a grandmother gave me new life; I saw it differently. I saw it through the eyes of a child. Rebecca had her father's dark eyes and hair but, otherwise, resembled her mother. From an early age, Rebecca loved the outdoors. After learning to crawl, we often followed her until she ended up sitting in front of the door—waiting to be taken out. When outside, she would stretch her tiny hands toward the leaves or wiggle until we would place her in the grass to crawl and explore on her own. She enjoyed books and pictures in general. Her grandfather Dan's picture along with her great, great, great grandmother Fannie's picture were on the wall of our great room along with her parents' and other family pictures. Rebecca would point and speak in baby-babble while Eli and Sarah offered a little family history.

The birthday club continued to meet monthly in an atmosphere of fun and laughter. Remembering old times was becoming a topic of interest. Who could remember the best stories? Jeanne, one of the members, moved to the country several miles from my home. It was a beautiful acreage with woodlands and a creek flowing through. During the summer months, we looked forward to morning coffees on Wednesdays.

I led a Bible study group, taught first aid classes, and continued with my volunteer work at Good Samaritan Rehab Center. And, I no longer felt uncomfortable around Martin. He would shake my hand whenever I came, and before I left, he would inevitably state, "Karen, I'm sorry. For your loss. Your husband. He died, didn't he? Was it the river?"

Simply answering, "Thank you, Martin. See you next time," satisfied him. One day, after finishing a game of rummy with Wilbur and Lilly, I lingered. Martin stared at his hands.

"Martin." It felt strange saying his name. I really had not had to use it during my volunteer activities. He looked up at me.

"Do you ever see Margo and her family?"

"My sister."

"Yes, your sister. Do you miss her?"

"Miss her?"

"Yes. Do you wish she could come more often?"

"It doesn't matter."

"She loves you very much. And, your parents do, too, although it's difficult for them to come."

He looked out the window.

"She wanted you to know. Family is important. You have a good family, and they do love and care for you."

He returned to look at his folded hands. With the usual screech of the chair, I stood to leave.

"Karen, I'm sorry. For your loss. Your husband. He died, didn't he. Was it the river?" Walking to a position behind his chair, I placed one arm around him and lightly hugged his shoulders. As a young college student, I had been first impressed with Martin's abundant self-esteem and sense of power. Though once strong and handsome, had he ever been capable? His biology and experiences had contaminated him somehow and left him diminished in a way and for reasons his loved ones would never understand.

"Martin, do you know where the chapel is here at the home?" I asked him.

He didn't answer. I remembered when we were married he said his faith was personal, not something to be talked about, and, no, he would not pray with me.

I left him with, "My prayers are with you."

When I arrived home that afternoon, I picked up Jerry Sittzer's book, A Grace Disguised, and read, "There are visible signs of behavior that manifest an unforgiving heart underneath—signs alerting us to the problem and warning us that something is happening in our souls."

38

As the years passed, it was natural that the family started referring to things as "before Dan died," and "after Dan died." This was soon lovingly shortened to BD and AD—usually stated with a soft smile of remembrance.

Eli had had foresight when he took me to the river that chilly November day after Dan died. The decision to stay in our home came easily after the first few months. The view from our home on the bluffs overlooking the Mississippi River was breathtaking. Nature often beckoned me. A bird's flight, a fish jumping out of the water, a deer in our woods got me outside often. As the years passed, the sights and sounds of nature became more precious: wild flowers and grasses, bird calls, the wind whipping through the trees, and the rush of river water. I wanted to share this with someone, Dan, but I knew he was in a more glorious place enjoying scenery I could not even imagine.

I traveled. I took an Alaskan cruise with a couple of friends. Bald eagles, whales, otters, glaciers carving incredible scenery, and the turquoise sea. It made me wonder if this spectacular view resembled creation. Pristine. Primitive. No houses, businesses, or other clutter covered the landscape. I saw nature at its best.

On another trip, I rode a bus to Washington, DC, with a group of veterans, Martin included. Our local chapter sponsored the trip and invited the veterans from the rehab center as long as a nurse and necessary volunteers accompanied them. We visited the Capitol and other historic sites; however, the main attraction was the Vietnam Veterans' Memorial with its 60,000 names. We touched the black granite wall and looked with interest at the mementos—hats, flags, pictures, boots placed near the wall. The conscientious objectors, those who serve, the veterans, the pacifists, the protestors all shared a common ground of grief. Finding the name of my high school sweetheart, Bill, and tenderly touching it, took me back decades to another time and place. Feeling the warmth of someone beside me, I turned to see Martin.

"Who is Bill?" he innocently asked.

"A friend. We were in high school together."

"Oh. I'm sorry. For your loss. Karen." The same words he used each week when I left.

"I'm sorry, too." I turned and gently took his hand as we walked back to the already full bus. On the ride home, there were questions I wanted to ask about his past, about our past together like whether he had taken the wedding pictures from my home. Yet, I felt he could not answer any of these questions. The question about the missing wedding pictures? Perhaps I didn't want the answer. The thought of Martin rummaging through my house and the need for him to have the pictures still troubled me. So, the ride home was quiet. A good quiet. The kind of quiet that feels grace-filled.

After our return from Washington, DC, I spent a lot of time crying. Always feeling like I needed to be strong, I had denied so many feelings in the past. I cried because I could and for all the times I didn't. Along with this, as the weeks and months passed, I grew more loving and compassionate. My heart went out to a young mother with too many burdens who happened to be grocery shopping on the same days as I and to an aging sister of the faith at Bible study with serious health problems who one morning described the kind of funeral she wanted.

I went home to plan my own funeral not because I intended to die, but Dan hadn't intended to die either. It was something we all needed to think about. Getting out a sheet of notebook paper, I wrote down my confirmation verse, the names of two of my favorite hymns, and a few other details. When it did happen it would be a celebration of life ceremony. Chocolate brownies with walnuts and ice cream would be served.

Pulling out a bottom drawer of my desk to store these spontaneous funeral plans, I noted the school report written decades ago about the Mississippi River. Where had time gone? And, here I was living on the very river I was mysteriously drawn to as a child. Also, an unfinished poem written years ago about forgiveness caught my attention. Re-reading, I knew I could complete it.

I can forgive. I can forgive.
With God's help, I can forgive.
I chipped away at the resentment
In the cold dark corner of my heart.

I can forgive; I can forgive.
With God's help, I can forgive.
Until the cold dark corner softened.
And there was nothing.
Nothing.

A still voice interrupted my weary thoughts with
Forgive yourself and you will have everything.
Everything:
Love.

Rubbing my temples after a long day but feeling content with a Praise be to God on my lips, I returned the finished poem to the bottom of the drawer with my funeral plans and childhood report about the Mighty Mississippi, took a warm bath, and prepared for bed. Watching the evening news, I learned the Pope had died and a selection process would begin. Sports, weather, local news—I started to grow drowsy and punched off on the remote. Pulling the couch quilt over me, wanting to warm up before I headed to bed, I gazed out the large windows facing the river.

It was April. A thunderstorm was brewing. Lightning struck. The darkness could no longer hide the trees and grasses as they whipped their limbs back and forth in frenzy. I loved storms. Even as a child I had wanted to be outside during a thunderstorm watching, listening, feeling. Flipping off the quilt and slipping into slippers, I padded to the deck doors and opened them. Sharp winds opened my robe, rushed over exposed skin, and scattered newspapers on the table behind me. Stepping outside, I closed the doors behind me, re-wrapped my robe and walked carefully down the steps to the dock. Lightning occasionally lit my path. Water slapped over the dock with wind's encouragement. I stopped occasionally to look up and out and to take in the storm.

Reaching the end of the dock, I searched the sky. Like a cannon, thunder punctuated the night and announced something of significance. Would the storm blow over or burst forth spilling its contents into the river and everything surrounding? Lowering my gaze, I searched the dark banks knowing they were a treasure store for shattered relics of past cultures. Dust to dust. Ancient fish bones, fossils, and more. What was once life was no more. Fannie came to mind, the beautiful Indian maiden who left the river for love and, then, returned to stay. And Dan....

Watching the river dance and swell with the storm's beat, I dropped to my knees in prayer. Feeling truly blessed, I gave praise to an awesome

173

God, the God of all creation, yet a God, who had a plan for me, who truly loved and cared for me. Feeling strengthened by prayer and the power of the storm, I stood and once again studied The Father of Waters remembering what Dan had once said. I've always wanted to look at the Mississippi where it flows into the sea…. As the heavens opened drenching me in rain, I remembered with some anticipation seeing in our local paper an advertisement for Mississippi River Cruises.

Wanting to know more and getting soaked to the skin, I turned back to the house as I heard our small fishing boat knock repeatedly on the dock posts as the wind and waves whipped it about. Dropping to my knees to tauten the rope and attach the boat to the dock, I wiped the rain from my eyes and realized the boat was not empty. Terror gripped me as I studied something or someone large sitting on the middle seat covered with tarp. As the tarp crackled and moved about with the wind, a white knuckled hand appeared gripping the side of the boat. Out of breath from fear, I rose on trembling legs to run when the hand grabbed my ankle. Falling to my knees while scrambling to escape, I looked back to see a man's face tilted downward--his grip latched to my ankle.

Wanting to curse him, I said nothing. What was he doing out in the storm? Why was he in our fishing boat? Taking a few deep breaths, I sat back on my knees and looked up into the night. Rain pelted my face, but I could see the threatening clouds above as the thunder and lightening did their thing. Calming myself through prayer, I released his fingers one by one and said only, "Martin."

Looking at me for the first time with haunted soul, he murmured, "I'm scared."

Helping him from the boat, hand in hand we walked the length of the slippery dock fighting the pull and push of the wind as the rain continued to soak us up the steps, past the house, and into the garage. Opening the passenger door of my car, Martin sat without complaint. After helping him with his seat belt and grabbing the car keys and a few dry towels, we drove to town in silence.

After much apologizing by staff members and speculation as to who turned off the night alarm, I left the rehab center expecting Martin's usual good-byes of "Karen. I'm so sorry for your loss…" Instead he slumped with his chin on his chest. Perhaps embarrassed, or simply exhausted. As I turned to leave I heard him tenderly speak,

"Karen. I'm sorry. You're all I have."

I turned around, went back to where he sat and kneeled beside his chair. The window behind him displayed a night as dark as coal. I didn't know what to say. But, Martin did.

"What do I need to know?" He questioned.

"Know? About what?" I asked as the shivers spread down my spine.

"What do I need to know to be saved?" He looked at me then, and I knew he was soul serious.

"God loves you Martin. You need to know that," I began. He studied my face wanting more.

"We are all sinners. You. Me. Everyone. But, God paid the price for our sin when he died on the cross."

"Easter, right?" He asked.

"Yes. It was Easter."

I looked out the window, again, as the moon appeared behind a cloud. Round, yellow, and clear.

"There's more isn't there?" He wanted me to go on.

"Yes, there's more. Since we all have sinned, we need to ask God for forgiveness. Continually." And, then I sighed. Sin: such a human condition. "Like the farmer who picks up rocks in the spring, only to return next spring and see that there are more."

He shifted slightly in his chair and started a smile.

"Last of all, He wants us to live as His children." He squeezed my hand. I got up to leave and noticed a Bible on the lamp stand beside his chair. Opening it up to John 3:16, I placed the Bible on his lap and pointed to the verse.

I backed out of the room quietly as he read softly, "For God so loved the world, that he gave his only begotten Son, that whosoever believeth in him should not perish, but have everlasting life…"

39

Spring turned to summer. Over time I became known as the "flower lady," the "bird lady," and some even referred to me as "that river lady" in our neighborhood. Robert, my steadfast neighbor, continued to assist with errands and general upkeep. He was a real blessing. I visited my parents as often as I could; and Eli, Sarah, and Rebecca spent weekends at my house whenever they could get away. The natural things in life—hugs and kisses, smiles, warm conversation, friendship, walks, fishing, collecting shells—were the lubricant that provided a certain kind of tranquility.

Listening to the early morning news one day in August while fixing a veggie omelet, I learned of a Russian sub trapped 600 feet below the surface in the Pacific Ocean. Tangled in fishing net or cables, the mini sub with its crew of seven were stuck at the bottom of a black sea with dwindling air supply. Wondering what could possibly be going through their minds, I prayed for their safety.

Deep, black, entangled, fearful. My thoughts turned to Martin. Thinking of the emotional baggage that pulled him down to a deep, dark place which in turn separated him from those who loved him, I began to understand. He was the way he was. Was it his early childhood? Did it lie hidden in some unknown gene? It was not a choice he had made. There were no good answers to many things in life.

I was young and naïve when I married Martin and so tied up in my own pain that I was incapable of sympathy or empathy towards him. Compassionate? Having known Martin for such a short period of time and being attracted to him for all the wrong reasons, I was not compassionate. However, God was and is. He loves unconditionally, steadfastly and even sent his son to suffer and die that we might live eternally. Had God given me another chance? Was that why Martin kept showing up in my life?

What is love—really? It was easy to love Eli. He had melted my heart as a child and grown up to be my forever son. His wife, Sarah, and my granddaughter, Rebecca, caused me to smile just thinking about them. I wandered into the family room to the wall where our pictures hung to take another peek at Rebecca's wonderful child face and, of course, was drawn to the last portrait of Dan and me taken so long ago, yet, it seemed just yesterday the love of my life had been taken. It was both good and bad to think of him; bad, because it hurt so much. The tears were for joy and without-end grief. I loved him still.

And, then, there was the time-worn portrait of Fannie, my great grandmother, the beautiful Indian maiden who chose to leave the river and her family for love—a love that didn't last. Or, did it? I didn't know what was in her heart or Great Grandpa's for that matter. Did separation mean lack of love or simply the incapability of dealing with life and making a choice to go it on your own? A tattered obituary stored over the years told a story of a man shot in Mexico by a jealous husband—his obituary saying he was survived only by a son—my grandfather.

In elementary school, we had learned of Pocahontas. The English thought of her as an Indian princess. She married John Rolfe, an English settler, and had a son who was educated in England and became a significant part of American history. Remember Sacagawea? She had a river, a peak, a mountain pass named after her. Monuments and memorials to her stand in Oregon, Montana, North Dakota and Idaho.

Fannie was not mentioned in the history books, and there are no monuments or memorials for her. I do not know where her burial ground is, but her spirit is part of my spirit, and I feel a love for her even though I never knew her. I rubbed her beautiful face with my fingers and wished I could go to a place and a time when I could have known her, spent time with her, felt the mystery of the river with her.

Although there were no pictures of Martin in my house, my thoughts were pulled again in his direction. He was so difficult to love and yet so needy of it.

On another morning in August as I hovered over a bowl of cold cereal, the National Weather Service field office in New Orleans issued a bulletin predicting catastrophic damage to New Orleans and the surrounding region. Approximately one million people fled the city and its surrounding suburbs due to Hurricane Katrina, failing flood walls and levees. Thunder predicted another rainy day. The river was swollen but not at a dangerous level.

Looking through my jewelry chest for my favorite earrings—a pair from grand-daughter Rebecca-- I brushed my hair quickly, applied some lip gloss, and dressed in jeans and a sweatshirt. Noting the earrings in the rearview mirror as I backed out of the garage—silver feathers dangling on a hoop—I remembered her sweet face and how delighted she was when I opened her gift. "Like your great grandmother," Rebecca smiled wanting me to understand.

At the end of our short driveway, I hopped out of the car to fetch the mail: a phone bill, a flyer from our local grocery, and a 5 x 7 worn-looking, manila envelope addressed to me in large child-like print. The envelope looked very familiar, but I couldn't place it. Getting back into the car, I used my house key to slice open one end of the envelope. Wedding pictures fell out revealing a much younger looking Martin standing beside a much younger looking Karen—wedding pictures taken years ago, stolen from my house, and now returned—yellow with age and covered with finger smudges.

Taking a deep breath and feeling somewhat annoyed, I tossed them in the back seat. Martin had kept these through the years. He wanted me to have them but was not able to return them to me in person. Heading to Jeanne's house for our weekly coffee, I could talk to her about this. Her perspective always helped. I turned on the CD player to one of my favorites: Charlie Pride's "Roll on Mississippi." I sang along as the windshield wipers swish-thunked, swish-thunked to the beat of the song. It was raining hard, and I noted in between wiper swishes that the trees and surrounding foliage were becoming saturated. We don't really need this, dear Lord, I thought.

Approaching Jeanne's place, I realized the creek had risen and covered a section of the long winding road leading to her home. No problem, I thought; the Jeep can handle it; I'll take it slow. Singing "Roll on Mississippi, you make me feel like a child, again," I put the Jeep in drive and started to creep forward.

After a few yards, the current took over. I stepped on the gas, then stepped on the brake and attempted to steer. None of it made a difference. I was drifting downstream away from Jeanne's house to a place I had never been. Choosing not to panic, I drifted along with a few tree limbs and other river debris hoping the jeep would be tossed on the opposite shore but it was sinking.

And I saw a new heaven and a new earth: for the first heaven and the first earth were passed away; and there was no more sea.....and God shall wipe away all tears from our eyes; and there shall be no more death, neither sorrow, nor crying, neither shall there be any more pain: for the former things are passed away...And He said unto me, It is done...

You were there. We walked hand in hand down to the dock you had so lovingly rebuilt. I pointed out the wildflowers bending with the breeze. You pointed out a fish wildly jumping with abandon near the end of the dock. You took me in your arms and there were no more tomorrows.

The Local Gazette

Jeep Upturns Causing Death

Karen Wilson accidentally drowned when her Jeep overturned in creek waters on Jesup Road. The Jeep was carried downstream and discovered by a local farmer soon after the accident. An autopsy determined that Ms. Wilson suffered a severe concussion which may have prevented her from trying to exit from the vehicle. She is survived by one son, Eli Wilson, his wife, Sarah, and grand daughter, Rebecca.

. . . .

Epilogue

After packing lightly, Eli and Sarah headed north in the wee hours of the morning. Rebecca, taken from her warm bed, strapped in her car seat with her favorite blanket, soon fell back asleep. Eli and Sarah spoke softly—remembering Karen. Remembering Dan. Remembering his own mother, and then asking Sarah, "Do you want to hear the story of Fannie, again?"

So much had happened. Listening to Rebecca's sleepy sounds, they touched hands and thanked God for what they had—each other.

Arriving at their destination later in the day, somewhat tired and weary, they parked their car and headed toward the lake. Lake Itasca. Trees whispered softly as the sun peeked into bits of their private conversations. Rebecca, carried by her mother, struggled to get down wanting to wet her feet. Goosebumps formed on her chubby child legs. Sarah wished she had dressed her in warmer clothes instead of the plaid, aqua colored shorts and bright pink tee shirt Rebecca had chosen the night before. Eli took a few pictures of a family filled with sorrow except for Rebecca who delighted in her surroundings. The trees, the water, the bird's song—she laughed gleefully.

Eli took the pot of ashes he had carried from the car, removed the lid, and scattered a few ashes across the lightly lapping waves.

"All the rivers run into the sea, yet the sea is not full; unto the place from whence the rivers come, thither they return again," he quietly spoke as he scattered another handful of his mother's ashes.

As they returned to the car, Rebecca's eyes focused on the water as she looked over her mother's shoulder—drawn to the mystery of the river.

"Did you know," Eli asked, "that a raindrop falling into Lake Itasca would arrive at the Gulf in about ninety days?" .

In Revelations,

God gives John a vision of what heaven will be like.

Heaven is pictured as a Holy City with

a river flowing through it…*

*(Taken from the Daily Bible, New International Version, Harvest House Publishers and the Zondervan Corporation, 1984.)

Notes:

Scripture references taken from the Holy Bible, Revised Standard Version, Thomas Nelson and Sons, New York, 1953.

Scripture references taken from the Good News Testament, American Bible Society, 1976 (The New Testament in Today's English Version).

Google: CNN.com

Google: Wikipedia

"Look for God's Way," by Ted Derrick, Faith Partners, Lynchburg, VA, June 1983 (see page 135)

Messiah Lutheran Church bulletin, Brownsburg, IN, July 23, 2007 (see page 157)

Sermon notes used from Augsburg Publishing House, 1982 (see page 169)

"Knowing God's Will" Bible study series, Stonecroft, Inc., Kansas City, Missouri.

www.ingramcontent.com/pod-product-compliance
Lightning Source LLC
Chambersburg PA
CBHW020411290526
45785CB00002B/503